GRADE 4

ommon CORE Comprehension

Practice at 3 Levels ●●●

Table of Contents

Using This Book **2**

Overview I • Introduction to Narrative Texts **6**

Unit 1: Personal Narratives Mini-Lesson **8**
Personal Narratives I **10**
Personal Narratives II **14**
Unit 2: Realistic Fiction Mini-Lesson **18**
Realistic Fiction I **20**
Realistic Fiction II **24**
Unit 3: Historical Fiction Mini-Lesson **28**
Historical Fiction I **30**
Historical Fiction II **34**
Unit 4: Trickster Tales Mini-Lesson **38**
Trickster Tales I **40**
Trickster Tales II **44**
Unit 5: Pourquoi Tales Mini-Lesson **48**
Pourquoi Tales I **50**
Pourquoi Tales II **54**

Overview II • Introduction to Informational Texts **58**

Unit 6: Social Studies Mini-Lesson **60**
Civilizations of the Americas **62**
Geography and Climate **66**
Economics **70**
Native Americans **74**
Unit 7: Science Mini-Lesson **78**
Life Science: Organisms **80**
Life Science: Classification **84**
Earth Science **88**
Physical Science **92**

Overview III • Introduction to Opinion/Argument **96**

Unit 8: Persuasive Letters Mini-Lesson **98**
Persuasive Letters I **100**
Persuasive Letters II **104**
Unit 9: Film/Book Reviews Mini-Lesson **108**
Film Reviews **110**
Book Reviews **114**
Unit 10: Advertisements Mini-Lesson **118**
Advertisements I **120**
Advertisements II **124**

Answer Key **128**

D1213576

Using This Book

What Is the Common Core?

The Common Core State Standards are an initiative by states to set shared, consistent, and clear expectations of what students are expected to learn. This helps teachers and parents know what they need to do to help students. The standards are designed to be rigorous and pertinent to the real world. They reflect the knowledge and skills that our young people need for success in college and careers.

What Are the Intended Outcomes of Common Core?

The goal of the Common Core Standards is to facilitate the following competencies. Students will:

- demonstrate independence;
- build strong content knowledge;
- respond to the varying demands of audience, task, purpose, and discipline;
- comprehend as well as critique;
- value evidence;
- use technology and digital media strategically and capably;
- come to understand other perspectives and cultures.

What Does This Mean for You?

If your state has joined the Common Core State Standards Initiative, then as a teacher you are required to incorporate these standards into your lesson plans. Your students may need targeted practice in order to meet grade-level standards and expectations, and thereby be promoted to the next grade. This book is appropriate for on-grade-level students as well as intervention, ELs, struggling readers, and special needs students. To see if your state has joined the initiative, visit http://www.corestandards.org/in-the-states.

What Does the Common Core Say Specifically About Reading?

For reading, the Common Core sets the following key expectations.

- Students must read a "staircase" of increasingly complex texts in order to be ready for the demands of college or career-level reading.
- Students must read a diverse array of classic and contemporary literature from around the world, as well as challenging informational texts in a range of subjects.
- Students must show a "steadily growing ability" to comprehend, analyze, and respond critically to three main text types: Argument/Opinion, Informational, and Narrative.

Common Core Comprehension Grade 4 • ©2012 Newmark Learning, LLC

How Does This Book Help My Students?

Common Core Comprehension offers:

- **Three leveled, reproducible versions of each passage** are provided so that below-grade-level students start their comprehension practice at their reading level. Repeated readings and teacher support scaffold students up to the on-grade-level passage. Struggling students do not miss out on essential comprehension practice because the comprehension questions can be answered no matter which passage is read. The Common Core Standards require students to progress to grade-level competency. Therefore, it is recommended that once students build background on the topic, they staircase up to the on-grade-level passage, which includes richer vocabulary and language structures.

  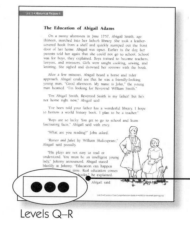

Levels L–M   Levels N–P   Levels Q–R

Gives the teacher the reading level of each of the three passages. See the chart on page 5.

- **An Overview page** introduces each of the three sections and provides background on the text type and genres in that section. A graphic organizer is provided to help you introduce the text type.

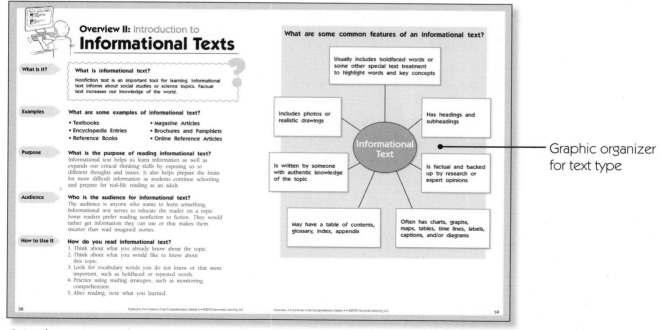

Graphic organizer for text type

Introductory spread

- **Each set of passages in a genre begins with a mini-lesson** that consistently frames the specific details of the genre students are about to read. A reproducible graphic organizer is provided for you to share as is, or you can cover the answers and complete together or individually as a response to your mini-lesson.

Explanation of the genre

Graphic organizer to copy or project

Brief explanation of how this text is different from other types of text

Gives a purpose for this genre

Notes the audience for this type of text

Tips for comprehending this type of text

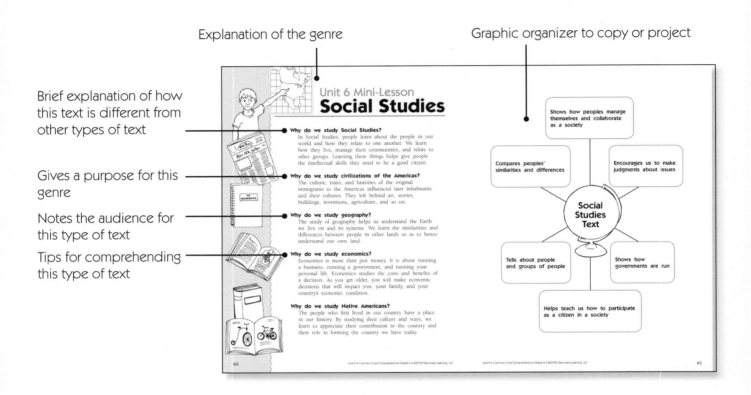

- **Text-dependent and critical-thinking questions** appear after each set of passages. The questions are research based and support the Common Core reading standards at grade level.

- **Students get rich text type and genre practice** using an array of narrative texts, content-area informational texts in social studies and science, and opinion/argument texts, as per the Common Core Standards.

Narrative Texts

Informational Texts

Opinion/Argument Texts

- **Vocabulary is studied in context,** as per the Common Core Standards.

> The Aztec had many gods and goddesses. The Aztec believed their gods ruled **agriculture**. Agriculture is farming. The Aztec wanted to make the gods happy. They thought if the gods were happy, crops would grow well.
>
> The Aztec believed their gods needed blood to be strong. The priests gave the gods human blood. They did this by killing

How Are the Passages Leveled?

The first passage is two grades below level, the second passage is one grade below level, and the third passage is on grade level. Please refer to the chart below to see a correlation to letter levels and number levels.

Common Core Practice Reading Levels

Level Icon	Grade 1		Grade 2		Grade 3		Grade 4		Grade 5		Grade 6	
●○○	A–C	1–4	D–E	5–8	F–I	9–16	L–M	24–28	N–P	30–38	Q–R	40
●●○	D–E	5–8	F–I	9–16	J–M	18–28	N–P	30–38	Q–R	40	S–U	44–50
●●●	F–I	9–16	J–M	18–28	N–P	30–38	Q–R	40	S–U	44–50	V–X	60

Overview I: Introduction to
Narrative Texts

What Is It?

What is a narrative text?

A narrative text is a real or fiction story that follows a story structure. That structure leads with capturing the reader's attention with an exciting or interesting beginning. The author then gives details about the characters, setting, and the plot. Usually a problem will arise, and suspense over what will happen occurs. Finally, there is a solution of the problem.

Examples

What are some examples of a narrative text?

- Fairy Tales
- Fables
- Tall Tales
- Mysteries
- Fantasy
- Historical Fiction
- Narrative Nonfiction
- Biographies
- Memoirs

Purpose

What is the purpose of a narrative text?

Basically, the purpose is to tell a story. Different types of narratives will have different purposes. For example, the purpose of a fable is to teach people lessons or explain mysteries of Earth.

Audience

Who is the audience for a narrative text?

The audience is any reader of that text. Although many people prefer certain types of narrative text to others, the stories are meant to interest anyone. Sometimes you will enjoy a story that is told really well, even though the story line is not your favorite.

How to Use It

How do you read a narrative text?

1. Read from beginning to end.
2. Use a graphic organizer to keep the characters straight.
3. Do research on real-life settings, if they are unfamiliar.

What are some common features of a narrative text?

Includes a problem with some suspense as to what will happen

Offers details about characters, setting, and plot

Has an exciting or interesting beginning

Narrative Text

Ends with a clear conclusion to the story

Contains actions that lead to a solution of the problem

Has a main event that has action and emotion

Unit 1 Mini-Lesson
Personal Narratives

What is a personal narrative?

A personal narrative is a nonfiction text that recreates an experience from the author's life. A personal narrative has a strong point of view, usually in the first person. It also communicates a distinct mood, or overall feeling. Most personal narratives are about something "big" in the author's life.

What is the purpose of a personal narrative?

A personal narrative is a way to describe an experience so that others feel as if they were there. Writers do this by using sensory details—what they saw, heard, touched, smelled, and tasted—and by including important events, characters, and dialogue.

How do you read a personal narrative?

1. The title will likely give you a clue about the experience that the author will describe.
2. Pay close attention to the sequence of events.
3. Ask yourself: *Did this event happen to the person, or did the person make it happen?*
4. Consider how this event affected the person's life.
5. Ask yourself: *Is the author writing to entertain, or is there something that I can learn from his or her experience?*

Who writes a personal narrative?

Everyone does! People record their experiences in diaries and journals, and share them in letters and e-mails. These informal writing opportunities provide valuable practice in selecting just the right details to make the experience come alive for others. A personal narrative includes specific details about the time, place, and people involved.

May be a few paragraphs or several pages in length

Includes the author's thoughts and feelings as well as the actual events

Focuses on one particular incident in the author's life

Personal Narrative

Uses sensory details—seeing, hearing, touch, smell, taste

Includes dialogue

Mission Beach, San Diego

My family pulled the car into the parking lot. It was sandy! That's because we were at the beach in San Diego, California. I jumped out of the black convertible. That's a car with a top that can be put down. It was cool of my dad to get such an awesome car for our vacation. I pulled out a red beach bag. I carried it to a sunny spot. The view was amazing: white sand and crystal blue water. *This place is ten times nicer than in Corpus Christi, Texas,* I thought. (That was the only other beach I had been to. That beach was a trash can compared with this beach. The water there was brownish and filled with seaweed. Yuck!)

I grabbed a pair of goggles and a snorkel. A snorkel is a tube that lets you breathe underwater. I had never snorkeled before. The mask made my head pull to one side. The weather was perfect. It was hot enough to go swimming, but not too hot to be outside.

Under me I saw a beautiful coral reef. A coral reef is made of skeletons from sea animals. It looked like a picture in a magazine. It was bright yellow and pink. There were lots of fish swimming in schools. Schools are groups of fish. I was dazzled, or amazed, by the bright colors. Some of the fish swam right up to me. One tiny fish swam right over my hand. The rubbery flippers tickled my hand. It felt so weird. I loved watching the coral reef move from side to side. Floating in the water was very relaxing. I felt very peaceful.

After a while, I got tired swimming. I took a clamshell to show my parents. The clamshell was the size of a half-dollar. I still have that clamshell. It reminds me of my adventure on that beach. It reminds me of how lucky I am to have been there.

Mission Beach, San Diego

My family pulled the car into the sandy parking lot. We were at the beach in San Diego, California. I jumped out of the black convertible that my dad drove with the top down. It was very cool of my dad to rent such an awesome car for our vacation. I got out a big, red beach bag. I carried it to a sunny spot and set up a place for us to sit. I looked around at the white sand and the crystal blue water. *This place is ten times nicer than in Corpus Christi, Texas,* I thought. (That was the only other beach I had been to. Compared with here, that beach was a trash can. The water there was brownish and filled with seaweed. Yuck!)

I grabbed a snorkel and a pair of goggles. I had never snorkeled before. The mask made my head tilt, or pull to one side. But I didn't care. The weather was perfect. I put my face in the water.

Under me I saw a beautiful coral reef. A coral reef is made of skeletons from sea animals. It looked like a picture in a magazine. It was full of bright neon yellows and pinks. There were a ton of fish swimming in schools, or groups. I was dazzled, or amazed, by the bright colors. Some of the fish swam right up to me. One tiny fish swam over my hand. I loved watching the coral reef sway, or move from side to side. Floating in the current, or moving water, was very relaxing. I had never felt so peaceful.

I took a clamshell to show my parents. The clamshell was the size of a half-dollar. It was different from the other shells I collected because it opened and closed.

I still have that clamshell. It reminds me of my adventure. It takes me back to that day on the beach. It reminds me of how lucky I am to have been there.

Mission Beach, San Diego

My family and I pulled into the sandy parking lot at the beach. I jumped out of the car, a black convertible that my dad drove with the top down. It was very cool of my dad to rent such an awesome car for our vacation in San Diego, California. I opened the trunk and I got out a big, red beach bag. I took in the view of the white sand and the crystal blue water. *This place is ten times nicer than in Corpus Christi,* I thought. (That was the only other beach I had been to, in Texas. Compared with here, that beach was a trash can. The water there was brownish and filled with seaweed. Yuck!) Then I grabbed a snorkel and a pair of goggles and headed for the Pacific Ocean.

I had never snorkeled before. The mask made my head tilt. I put my face in the water and opened my eyes. Under me I saw a beautiful coral reef. It looked like a picture in a magazine. It was full of bright neon yellows and pinks. There were tons of fish swimming in schools. I couldn't believe fish came in so many different shapes, sizes, and patterns. I was dazzled by the bright colors. Some of the fish swam right up to me. One tiny fish swam right over my hand. It felt so weird how the rubbery flippers tickled my hand.

I loved watching the coral reef sway from side to side. It was so relaxing, almost hypnotic, floating with the gentle current. The warm water lapped against my cold body. I had never felt so peaceful.

I grabbed a clamshell to show my parents and swam back to shore. The clamshell was the size of a half-dollar. It was different from the other shells I collected because I could open and close it. I still have that clamshell. It reminds me of my adventure. It takes me back to that day on the beach. It reminds me of how lucky I am to have been there.

Name _____ Date _____

Use what you read in the passage to answer the questions.

1. Where does this narrative take place?

_____

_____

2. What kind of car is the family driving? Why does the writer think it was awesome?

_____

_____

3. How is Mission Beach different from the beach in Corpus Christi?

_____

_____

4. Has the writer ever snorkled before? How do you know?

_____

_____

5. What does the coral reef look like?

_____

_____

6. What clues help you conclude that the fish are not afraid of swimmers?

_____

_____

7. The clamshell is the size of what?

_____

_____

8. How does the writer feel about the trip? How can you tell?

_____

_____

Lucy

I listened to my mom on the phone. "Yes, Doug. I think you should come home. You need to say good-bye." Oh gosh. Why would my dad need to come home from his business trip? Then my mom came in and sat down next to me.

"Lucy feels bad and the medicine isn't working. Her back hurts. She hasn't gotten up in days." Not my dog! I have had Lucy since she was four. Now she was ten and a half.

"Your father and I have been thinking that maybe we should put her to sleep so she isn't in so much pain." I knew "put to sleep" meant to die.

I started to cry. "No! Mom, you can't! Take her to the vet." A vet is an animal doctor. Lucy's vet is Dr. Malden. "Maybe Dr. Malden has other ideas. Please." I begged.

Mom was quiet for a moment. Then she said, "I'll take her to the vet. But I was talking with your father just now. I suggested he should fly home from Boston so he can say good-bye to Lucy." I went to bed that night feeling horrible.

The next day at school was terrible. The whole time I was praying that Lucy would be okay. When I got home, my mom was cheerful. "Katie, guess what?" she asked. "I took Lucy to the vet. It wasn't easy, either. Your sister helped me lift her into the car. Then an assistant at the vet's office had to carry Lucy in. But when Lucy saw Dr. Malden, she jumped to her feet. She ran right to him! Dr. Malden said, 'Why did you bring this dog here? She's so active.'"

We went to my bedroom. Mom opened the door. Can you guess who was there with her tail wagging? Lucy! I was SO glad to see her! I hugged my furry pal for a long time.

Lucy

I listened to my mom on the phone. "Yes, Doug. I think you should come home to say good-bye." Then she hung up. Why would my dad need to come home from his business trip?

"Katie, Lucy isn't in the best shape and the medicine isn't working. Her back still hurts her. She hasn't gotten up in two days. Your father and I have been thinking that maybe we should put her to sleep so she isn't in so much pain."

What? Not my dog! I have had my dog Lucy since she was four. Now she was ten and a half. Then I started to cry. "NO! Take her to the vet." The vet is the doctor that takes care of animals. "Maybe Dr. Malden has some other ideas."

Mom was quiet for a moment. Then she said, "I'll take her to the vet. But I was talking with your father. I said he should fly home to say good-bye." My mom was sad, too. I went to bed that night feeling horrible.

The next day at school was terrible. I was sulking, or acting angry and quiet. I didn't even feel like playing during recess. When I got home, something weird was going on. My mom looked joyful.

"Katie, guess what?" she asked. "I took Lucy to the vet like you asked. It wasn't easy, either. I needed your sister to help me lift her into the car. At the vet's office, one of the assistants had to carry Lucy in. As soon as Lucy saw Dr. Malden, she jumped to her feet. Can you believe that?"

We went to my bedroom. Mom opened the door. Can you guess who was there, tail wagging? Lucy! I cried. I hugged my furry old pal for a long, long time.

Lucy

I was at home doing my homework when I heard my mom on the phone. "Yes, Doug. I think you should come home to say good-bye." Then she hung up. Oh gosh. Why would my dad need to come home from his business trip? I had no time to think because my mom came into my room.

"As you know, Lucy isn't in the best shape, and the medicine we're giving her isn't working. She's still having terrible back problems. She hasn't gotten up in two days. We have been thinking that we should put her to sleep."

"No! Mom, you can't! NO! Take her to the vet. See if Dr. Malden can recommend anything else. Please."

Mom was quiet for a moment. "I'll take her to the vet. But I was talking with your father, and I suggested he should fly home from Boston and say good-bye." I could see that Mom was sad, too. I went to bed that night feeling horrible.

The next day at school was dreadful. If I wasn't thinking about her, I was sulking. I rode home on the school bus praying that Lucy would be okay. When I got home, my mom looked joyful. How could she be happy at a time like this?

"Katie, guess what?" she said. "I took Lucy to the vet like you asked. It wasn't easy, either. I needed your sister to help me lift her into the car. One of the assistants had to carry Lucy into the office. But as soon as Lucy saw Dr. Malden, she jumped to her feet and ran right to him."

We went to my bedroom and Mom opened the door. Can you guess who was there, tail wagging? Lucy! I cried. I hugged my furry old pal for a long, long time. Then I brought her inside to play. And to think that I was worried.

Name _____ Date _____

Use what you read in the passage to answer the questions.

1. Who is Lucy?

_____

_____

2. What kind of trip is Katie's father on?

_____

_____

3. Why does Katie feel horrible when she goes to bed?

_____

_____

4. What is the name of the vet?

_____

_____

5. What kind of problem is Lucy having?

_____

_____

6. Why is it a challenge to get Lucy to the vet?

_____

_____

7. Where is Lucy when Katie gets home from school?

_____

_____

8. What clues help you conclude how Katie feels when she realizes Lucy is okay?

_____

_____

Realistic Fiction

What is realistic fiction?

Realistic fiction features characters and plots that could actually happen in everyday life. The settings are authentic—they are based on familiar places such as a home, school, office, or farm. The stories involve some type of conflict or problem. The conflict can be something a character faces within himself, an issue between characters, or a problem between a character and nature.

What is the purpose of realistic fiction?

Realistic fiction shows how people grow and learn, deal with successes and failures, make decisions, build relationships, and solve problems. In addition to making readers think and wonder, realistic fiction is entertaining. Most of us enjoy "escaping" into someone else's life for a while.

Who is the audience for realistic fiction?

Anyone is the audience for realistic fiction. Realistic fiction is especially enjoyable for readers who are interested in human thoughts, feelings, and experiences in a realistic place or circumstance.

How do you read realistic fiction?

First note the title. The title will give you a clue about an important character or conflict in the story. As you read, pay attention to the thoughts, feelings, and actions of the main characters. Note how the characters change from the beginning of the story to the end. Ask yourself: *What moves this character to action? Can I learn something from his or her struggles?*

Has at least one character who deals with a conflict (with self, others, or nature)

Takes place in a realistic setting

Has characters who are like people you might meet in real life

R₁ E₁ A₁ L₁ I₁ S₁ T₁ I₁ C₃
F₄ I₁ C₃ T₁ I₁ O₁ N₁

Is told from a first person point of view (I, me, my, we, etc.) or third person point of view (he, she, they, their)

Is not true but could happen

Luke and the Books

"Help!" shouted Luke. "I'm in serious trouble. I started my report. It's about nineteenth-century western pioneers. But the computer stopped working. Will you help me?" Luke asked.

"We're not going to do your work for you," warned Jamal.

"I'm not asking you to," said Luke. "My report needs to be two pages. If all of you tell me one thing you know, that should be enough for two pages." Luke took out a notebook. "I know pioneers rode in covered wagons."

"The pioneers used a spinning wheel to make thread. Then they weaved the thread into cloth," explained Brooke.

"I once saw a movie about pioneers. They built a barn together. It was a musical," said Tia. "They twirled, or spun, axes. They did gymnastics on piles of lumber."

"Oh! Oh! Pick me!" shouted Jalissa. "I read a book about a pioneer girl and her family. One time grasshoppers fell from the sky. They attacked the pioneers. They ate all the food." Luke wrote in his notebook.

"I don't have two pages. I need more facts!" Luke groaned.

"You need an encyclopedia. Then you can look up *pioneers*," Brooke suggested. "Encyclopedias are books that have information about a lot of different things." Luke was discouraged. The encyclopedia wasn't just one book. It was twenty-six! Luke thought he would drown in all that information.

"Don't worry," said Brooke. "There is one book for each letter of the alphabet. Use the book with the letter *p*."

Luke's friend helped him find the *P* book. He looked up *pioneer*. He looked at all the information. "Here are the grasshoppers. It says here they're called locusts." Luke worked on his report. Soon he wrote two pages. "I'm almost a pioneer myself now. I did my entire report without a computer!"

Luke and the Books

Help!" shouted Luke. "I'm in serious trouble," he said. "I started my report about nineteenth-century western pioneers. But the computer stopped working. Help me?" asked Luke.

"We're not going to do your work for you," warned Jamal.

"I'm not asking you to," said Luke. "I need to write a two-page report. If all of you of tell me one thing you know, that should be enough for two pages." Luke took out a notebook. "I know something about pioneers. I know they rode in covered wagons. Who else knows something?" he asked.

"The pioneers used a spinning wheel to make thread. Then they weaved the thread into cloth," explained Brooke.

"I once saw a movie about pioneers. They worked together to build a barn. It was a musical," said Tia.

"Oh!" shouted Jalissa. "I read a book about a pioneer girl and her family. In one part grasshoppers descended from the sky. They came down and attacked the pioneers. They ate their food." Luke wrote in his notebook.

"I don't have enough. I need more facts!" Luke groaned.

"You need to get an encyclopedia. Then you can look up *pioneers*," Brooke suggested. "Encyclopedias are books that have information." The encyclopedia wasn't just one book. It was twenty-six! Luke feared he would drown in all that information.

"There is a book for each letter of the alphabet. Use the book with the first letter of your topic," said Brooke.

Luke found the *P* book. He looked up *pioneer*. "Whoa!" he said happily. "Here are the grasshoppers. But it says here they are called locusts." Luke set to work. Soon he wrote his two pages. "I'm practically a pioneer myself now. I did my entire report without a computer!"

Luke and the Books

Help!" shouted Luke. "I started writing my report about nineteenth-century western pioneers—but the computer stopped working. You'll help me out, won't you?" asked Luke.

"We're not going to do your work for you," warned Jamal.

"I'm not asking you to," said Luke. "If I write down what all five of us know, it should be enough to make a two-page report." He opened the pad of paper. "Here's what I know: Pioneers rode in covered wagons. Now, who's next?"

"There was a spinning wheel the pioneers used to make thread they could weave into cloth," Brooke offered.

"I saw a movie musical where pioneers built a barn," offered Tia. "They twirled axes and did gymnastics."

"Oh!" shouted Jalissa. "I read a book about a pioneer girl and her family who lived on a prairie! My favorite part is where grasshoppers descend from the sky. They come down and attack the pioneers and eat all their food." Luke wrote more notes.

"This isn't going to be anywhere near two pages" groaned Luke.

"You need to get an encyclopedia and look up *pioneers*," Brooke advised. "Encyclopedias are books that have information about different things," Brooke informed him. To Luke's dismay, the encyclopedia wasn't just one book—it was twenty-six! He feared he would drown in the ocean of information.

"Don't worry. The books are divided by the letters of the alphabet," Brooke said.

Luke looked up *pioneer* in the *P* book. "Whoa!" he said happily. "Here are the grasshoppers but they're called locusts."

Luke set to work. Soon his two pages were written. "I'm practically a pioneer myself now. I did my report without a computer!"

Name _____ Date _____

Use what you read in the passage to answer the questions.

1. What is Luke's report about?

_____

_____

2. How does Jamal feel about helping Luke? How can you tell?

_____

_____

3. How long does Luke's report need to be?

_____

_____

4. What did the pioneers use to make thread for cloth?

_____

_____

5. Who saw a musical movie about pioneers?

_____

_____

6. What happened after the grasshoppers came down from the sky?

_____

_____

7. What clues help you conclude that this is Luke's first time using an encyclopedia?

_____

_____

8. How does Luke solve his problem?

_____

_____

Click-Clack, Who's There?

I really wanted to start a band. I told Linda my idea. She laughed. "Jake, no one we know plays an instrument."

"Maria plays the piano," I reminded her. "She has a battery-powered keyboard. It's **portable**. That means she can take it places. She can bring it to the cave."

Linda stopped laughing. "The cave?" she said. "But the cave makes a scary echo. What will we do about that?" asked Linda. The cave made her nervous.

"The cave will make the music seem softer and a little spooky. Our band will sound even better!" I said.

Cai loved the idea of a band. "I'll play my bongo drums." Maria loved the idea too.

"We're meeting at three. It might be a little dark, so I'll bring my flashlight," I said.

"All right, I'll bring my harmonica," Linda said. I had forgotten Linda played the harmonica! I had my band, but I had a problem. I couldn't play an instrument.

I still hadn't solved my problem as Linda and I headed toward the cave. My flashlight was a special miner's light. My father found the light a long time ago in a weird antique store. When we got to the cave, Cai and Maria were inside.

"Where's your instrument?" Maria asked me. I nervously turned my miner's light on and off, on and off. *Click-clack, click-clack*, went the switch.

"That's a great instrument!" Cai said. "I can hear the *click-clack* of your light turning on and off. It makes a cool sound and your light can keep time with the music." I realized my problem was solved. I flicked the light on and off. Before we knew it, we had our band!

Click-Clack, Who's There?

I really wanted to start a band. I told my sister Linda about my idea, and she laughed out loud. She said, "Jake, no one we know plays an instrument."

"Maria plays the piano," I reminded her. "She has a battery-powered keyboard. It's portable. She can bring it to the cave."

Linda stopped laughing. "The cave?" she said. "Caves make an echo. What will we do about that?" asked Linda. She didn't like the idea of the cave.

"The echo will make the band sound better," I said.

"Great idea!" said Cai. "I'll play my bongo drums. When do we start?" I knew Cai would like my idea.

"I'll go get my keyboard," Maria said happily.

"Let's meet at three. It might be a little dark, so I'll bring my flashlight," I said.

"Fine, I'll bring my harmonica," Linda said. I had forgotten about Linda's harmonica! Now I had my band, but I had a problem: I couldn't play an instrument.

Linda and I headed toward the cave. My flashlight was a special miner's light. My father found the light in a weird antique store. Cai and Maria were inside with their instruments. "Where's your instrument?" Maria asked me. I nervously flicked my miner's light on and off, on and off. *Click-clack, click-clack*, went the switch.

"That's a great instrument!" Cai said. "I can hear the *click-clack* of your light turning on and off. Not only does it make a cool sound, but your light can keep time with the music."

"Um, yeah!" I said, quickly realizing my problem was solved. I flicked the light on and off. We had our band!

Click-Clack, Who's There?

It's really hard to start a band, but I was determined. When I told Linda she said, "Jake, no one we know plays an instrument."

"Maria plays the piano," I reminded her. "And she has a portable, battery-powered keyboard that she can bring to the cave when we practice."

Linda stopped laughing. "The cave? What about the echoes?" Linda asked skeptically.

"The echoes will make the band sound even better," I said.

"I'll play my bongo drums. When do we start?" asked Cai. I knew Cai would like my idea. Maria was enthusiastic too.

"Let's meet at three. It might be a little dark, so I'll bring my flashlight," I said.

"Okay, I'll bring my harmonica," Linda said reluctantly. I had my band, but I also had a problem: I couldn't play an instrument! Linda and I headed toward the cave. My flashlight was a special miner's light that my father had found in a weird, old antique store.

Cai and Maria were inside with their instruments. "Where's your instrument?" Maria asked me. I nervously flicked my miner's light on and off, on and off, as I tried to think of something to say. *Click-clack, click-clack*, went the switch.

"That's a great instrument!" Cai said. "I can hear the *click-clack* of your flashlight. Not only does it make a cool sound, but your light can keep time with the music." Realizing my problem was solved, I flicked the flashlight on and off, and then Cai joined in with his bongos. Maria and Linda started to play, too. We had our band!

Name _____ Date _____

Use what you read in the passage to answer the questions.

1. What does the word **portable** mean?

_____

_____

2. What will Cai play in the band?

_____

_____

3. What is Jake's problem?

_____

_____

4. How does Linda feel about the cave? What clues helped you figure it out?

_____

_____

5. What effect does Jake think the echo will have?

_____

_____

6. Why does Jake bring his flashlight to the cave?

_____

_____

7. What is Jake's flashlight? Where did he get it?

_____

_____

8. How is Jake's problem solved?

_____

_____

Unit 3 Mini-Lesson
Historical Fiction

What is historical fiction?

Historical fiction stories take place in the past. Historical fiction stories have characters, settings, and events based on historical facts. The characters can be based on real people or made up. The dialogue is made up. But the information about the time period must be authentic, or factually accurate.

What is the purpose of historical fiction?

Historical fiction blends history and fiction into stories that could have actually happened. It adds a human element to history. Readers can learn about the time period: how people lived, what they owned, and even what they ate and wore. Readers can also see how people's problems and feelings have not changed much over time.

Who tells the story in historical fiction?

Authors usually write historical fiction in one of two ways. In the first person point of view, one of the characters tells the story as it happens to him or her, using words such as *I* and *our*. In the third person point of view, a narrator tells the story and refers to the characters using words such as *he* and *her*. The narrator may also refer to the characters by name.

How do you read historical fiction?

1. The title gives you a clue about an important time, place, character, or situation.
2. Note how the characters' lives compare with yours.

3. Note the main characters' thoughts, feelings, and actions, and how they change during the story.
4. Consider what you can learn today from people's struggles long ago.

Includes events that did or could have occurred in the setting

Takes place in an authentic historical setting

Has at least one character who deals with a conflict (self, others, or nature)

Historical Fiction

Has made-up dialogue but may be based on letters, a diary, or a report

Is told from a first person or third person point of view

Ponce de León and the True Fountain of Youth

My name is Alonzo Sanchez. I grew up on the island of Puerto Rico. Puerto Rico was one of the first Spanish colonies in the New World. I remember the day I met Ponce de León, the great explorer, and then the day he died. I was only ten years old. My family had signed on to be part of Ponce de León's farming colony. It was in a place he'd named Florida, the "land of flowers."

"In Florida, there is gold in the rivers," said a dark-haired girl. "Honey flows from the trees."

"You are forgetting the greatest treasure," said a man with a loud voice. It was Juan Ponce de León! His eyes twinkled. "There is a story about a spring," he said. "They say that an old person who swims in the water becomes young again."

Later that day, two ships set off for the unknown. Finally, we saw the west coast of Florida. We were there only a few days when Native Americans from the Calusa tribe attacked the colony. Ponce de León and the soldiers fought back. But there were more of them than us.

Our leader was shot with a poisoned arrow. I went to see Ponce de León. He was lying on his bed. He was sweating from a fever. I filled a cup with water. Ponce de León was dying. He said, "Ah, young Sanchez," and the old twinkle returned to his eyes. "Have you brought me the magic water? I will die otherwise."

"No, sir," I answered. "This is water from the rain barrel."

"It is good, Alonzo. Thank you. Promise me that you will keep looking for the fountain of youth."

I did not find a spring with magic waters. But if you live your life bravely, you will find the true fountain of youth.

Ponce de León and the True Fountain of Youth

My name is Alonzo Sanchez. I grew up on the island of Puerto Rico. I went into business as a coffee trader. Then I owned a plantation and built a hospital. I remember the day I met Ponce de León, the great explorer, and the day he died. I was ten years old. My family was part of Ponce de León's farming colony called Florida. It means "land of flowers."

"In Florida, there is gold in the rivers. Honey flows from the trees," said a dark-haired girl.

"You are forgetting the greatest treasure," a man's voice boomed. It was Juan Ponce de León! His eyes twinkled. "There is a story about a spring where the waters bubble up hot from underground," he said. "They say that an elderly person who swims in the water becomes young again."

Later that day, two ships set off for the unknown. Finally, we saw the west coast of Florida. Ponce de León and the other expedition picked a place by the mouth of a river to go ashore. Native Americans from the Calusa tribe attacked the colony. We retreated to the ships. Ponce de León and the soldiers fought back, but there were too many from the Calusa tribe. Our leader was shot with a poisoned arrow.

I went to give Ponce de León a cup of water. Ponce de León said hoarsely, "Ah, young Sanchez, have you brought me the magic water? I'm dying and I sure could use some."

"No, sir," I answered. "This is water from the rain barrel."

"It is good, Alonzo. Thank you. Now let me rest. Promise me that you will keep looking for the fountain of youth."

I did not find a spring with magic waters. But I found that if you go through life bravely, you will have found the true fountain of youth.

Ponce de León and the True Fountain of Youth

My name is Alonzo Sanchez. I grew up on the island of Puerto Rico. I went into business as a coffee trader. Eventually, I owned a plantation. I had a family. I built a hospital. But my thoughts go back many years, first to the day I met Ponce de León, the great explorer, and then to the day he died. I was only ten years old. My family had signed on to be part of Ponce de León's farming colony in a place he had named Florida, the "land of flowers."

"In Florida, there is gold in the rivers, and honey flows from the trees," said a dark-haired girl.

"You are forgetting the greatest treasure," a man's voice boomed. It was Juan Ponce de León! "There is a story about a spring," he said, "and they say that an elderly person who swims in the water becomes young. That is what I seek."

The two ships heavy with people and animals set off for the unknown. Finally, we saw land, the west coast of Florida. The colony was only a few days old when Native Americans from the Calusa tribe attacked. Ponce de León and the soldiers fought back, but they were outnumbered. Our leader was shot with a poisoned arrow. I went to see Ponce de León. I filled a cup with water. Ponce de León stared out dully. Then he said hoarsely, "Ah, young Sanchez," and the old twinkle returned to his eyes. "Have you brought me the magic water to rescue me from death?"

"No, sir," I answered. "This is water from the rain barrel."

"It is good, Alonzo. But promise me you will keep looking for the fountain of youth."

We did not find a spring with magic waters. But I did find that if you go forth bravely, you will have found the true fountain of youth.

Name _____ Date _____

Use what you read in the passage to answer the questions.

1. Who was Ponce de León?

_____

_____

2. What did Ponce de León name his farming colony?

_____

_____

3. What can you conclude about Alonzo Sanchez from the clues in this passage?

_____

_____

4. How old was Sanchez when Ponce de León died?

_____

_____

5. What is said to happen in the fountain of youth?

_____

_____

6. Who won the battle against the Calusa tribe? How do you know?

_____

_____

7. What clues help you conclude that Ponce de León liked Sanchez?

_____

_____

8. In what way did Sanchez find the real fountain of youth?

_____

_____

The Education of Abigail Adams

It was a sunny afternoon in June 1757. Thirteen-year-old Abigail Smith marched into her father's, William Smith's, library. She took a book from a shelf. Then she stomped out the front door. Earlier that day, Abigail's parents said she could not go to school. School was for boys, they explained. Boys trained to become teachers, doctors, and ministers. Girls were taught cooking, sewing, and knitting. She sighed and began to read the book.

After a few minutes, Abigail heard a horse and rider. He was a friendly-looking young man. He brought the horse to a stop a few yards away. "Good afternoon," the young man said with a smile. "My name is John. Where is the home of Reverend William Smith?"

"I'm Abigail. Reverend Smith is my father!" Abigail said.

"I hear that your father has a wonderful library, Abigail. I hope to borrow a world history book. You see, I plan to be a teacher."

"Boys are so lucky. You go to school and learn fascinating things," Abigail said sadly.

"What are you reading?" John asked.

"*Romeo and Juliet* by William Shakespeare," Abigail said proudly.

"His plays are not easy to read," John said. "You must be very smart. You have no problem!" Abigail felt confused. "Education can happen anywhere. It comes from reading books," he explained.

"I never thought of that," Abigail said.

The Education of Abigail Adams

On a sunny afternoon in June 1757, thirteen-year-old Abigail Smith marched into her father's library. She took a book from a shelf and stomped out the front door of her home in a fury. Earlier that day, Abigail's parents said she could not go to school. School was for boys. Boys trained to become teachers, lawyers, and ministers. Girls were taught cooking, sewing, and knitting at home. She sighed and began to read the book.

After a few minutes, Abigail heard a horse and rider. Abigail looked at the friendly-looking young man.

"Good afternoon," the young man said with a smile. "My name is John, and I'm looking for Reverend William Smith."

"My name is Abigail. Reverend Smith is my father! But he's not home right now," Abigail said happily.

"I hear that your father has a wonderful library, Abigail. I hope to borrow a book. You see, I plan to be a teacher."

"Boys are so lucky. You get to go to school and learn fascinating things," Abigail said with envy.

"What are you reading?" John asked.

"*Romeo and Juliet* by William Shakespeare," Abigail said proudly.

"His plays are not easy to read or understand. You must be an intelligent young lady," John replied. "Education can happen anywhere, at any time. Real education comes from reading lots of books," he explained.

"I never realized that," Abigail said.

The Education of Abigail Adams

On a sunny afternoon in June 1757, Abigail Smith, age thirteen, marched into her father's library. She took a leather-covered book from a shelf and quickly stomped out the front door of her home. Abigail was upset. Earlier in the day, her parents told her again that she could not go to school. School was for boys, they explained. Boys trained to become teachers, lawyers, and ministers. Girls were taught cooking, sewing, and knitting. She sighed and drowned her sorrows with the book.

After a few minutes, Abigail heard a horse and rider approach. Abigail could see that he was a friendly-looking young man. "Good afternoon. My name is John," the young man beamed. "I'm looking for Reverend William Smith."

"I'm Abigail Smith. Reverend Smith is my father! But he's not home right now," Abigail said.

"I've been told your father has a wonderful library. I hope to borrow a world history book. I plan to be a teacher."

"Boys are so lucky. You get to go to school and learn fascinating facts," Abigail said with envy.

"What are you reading?" John asked.

"*Romeo and Juliet* by William Shakespeare," Abigail said proudly.

"His plays are not easy to read or understand. You must be an intelligent young lady," Johnny announced. Abigail stared blankly at Johnny. "Education can happen anywhere, at any time. Real education comes from reading lots of books," he explained.

"I never thought of that," Abigail said enthusiastically.

Name _____ Date _____

Use what you read in the passage to answer the questions.

1. What year is it in this story?

_____

_____

2. What clues in the first paragraph help you infer that Abigail is in a bad mood?

_____

_____

3. How are Abigail and her father alike?

_____

_____

4. Why is Abigail upset by what her parents told her?

_____

_____

5. What book is Abigail reading when she meets John?

_____

_____

6. Why is John looking for the Smiths' house?

_____

_____

7. Why does Abigail say to John that boys are lucky?

_____

_____

8. What clues help you draw the conclusion that Abigail likes John?

_____

_____

Trickster Tales

What is a trickster tale?

A trickster tale is a short story in which animals or other creatures talk, think, and act like people. One character, the trickster, uses clever pranks or traps to fool another character. Often the trickster is much smaller than the character he fools. Sometimes the trickster wants to help others, but other times the trickster wants to help only himself.

What is the purpose of a trickster tale?

A trickster tale shows human characteristics and problems in an entertaining way. A trickster tale often teaches a lesson. The tale shows what happens when people make bad choices—although some of the bad choices come from the tricksters themselves!

How do you read a trickster tale?

Pay attention to the title. The title will often tell you which character is the trickster. Each character stands for ways that humans behave. As you read, ask yourself: *What human quality, or trait, does each character represent?* Notice what happens to the main characters. Think about how the events in the story support the lesson that the tale tries to teach

Who invented trickster tales?

Trickster tales originated all over the world, but African and Native American tales are among the most common today. The tales were originally passed down through oral storytelling. In modern times, many have been made into books and films. Some of today's popular cartoon characters are tricksters!

Has main characters that are usually animals

Is short and usually funny

Has a trickster, sometimes with a flaw

Trickster Tale

Ends with the trickster outwitting another character to solve the problem

Features a problem and a solution

Coyote Brings Fire to the People

Long ago, the only fire in the world was on a mountaintop. Three **selfish** Skookums lived there. The Skookums were big, scary beings. They wouldn't share the fire with anyone. The Skookums did not care if humans suffered during the icy, cold winter.

Coyote felt sorry for the people. He decided he would take some fire from the Skookums and bring it to the people. He asked Squirrel, Chipmunk, and Frog to help. The four animals went to the mountain where the Skookums lived. The Skookums seemed to be asleep. So Coyote grabbed a flaming branch of fire. He ran!

Unfortunately, one of the Skookums was not quite asleep. He let out a very loud screech. They ran after Coyote. Coyote went fast as lightning down the mountain. But the Skookums were faster. One stretched out a claw-like hand to stop him. Its fingers closed on the tip of Coyote's tail.

Coyote shouted when he felt the Skookum touch him. He tossed the fire to Squirrel. Squirrel caught the burning branch. As Squirrel leapt from tree to tree, the fire burned her back. Her tail curled up from the pain. She threw the fire down to Chipmunk. As the Skookums got closer, Chipmunk tossed the fire to Frog. Frog caught the fire in his mouth. Then he spat the fire out onto a piece of wood. The wood swallowed the fire.

The Skookums stood around the wood. They knew the fire was inside the wood. They did not know how to get it out. The Skookums screeched with anger. Then they left.

Clever Coyote knew how to get the fire out of the wood. He knew that if blazing fire could shrink to a tiny ember, then a spark can grow into a blazing fire. Coyote showed the people how to make fire by rubbing two dry sticks together. From that time on, people knew how to get fire out of wood.

Coyote Brings Fire to the People

Long ago, the only fire in the world was on a mountaintop. Three selfish Skookums lived there. The Skookums did not care if humans suffered during the icy, cold winter.

Coyote felt sorry for the people. He decided he would take some fire from the Skookums and bring it to the people. He asked Squirrel, Chipmunk, and Frog to help. Late at night, the four animals went to the mountain where the Skookums lived. The Skookums looked as if they had nodded off to sleep. Coyote grabbed a flaming branch from the fire—and ran!

Unfortunately, one of the Skookums was not quite asleep. They all ran after Coyote with menace in their eyes. One Skookum stretched out a claw-like hand to stop him.

When Coyote felt the Skookum's touch, he shouted and tossed the fire to Squirrel. As Squirrel leapt from tree to tree, the fire scorched, or burned, her back. She threw the fire down to Chipmunk. The Skookums rushed toward Chipmunk. Chipmunk tossed the fire to Frog. Frog caught the fire in his mouth.

By now the fire had shrunk to a small, glowing ember. Frog spat the fire out onto a piece of wood. The wood swallowed the fire, and it disappeared.

The Skookums were confused. They shrieked at the wood. The wood did not give up the fire. Finally, screeching with anger, the Skookums went back to their mountaintop.

Clever Coyote knew how to get the fire out of the wood. Just as a blazing fire can shrink to a tiny ember, a spark can grow into a blazing fire. Coyote showed the people how to rub two dry sticks together to make sparks. From that time on, people knew how to get fire out of wood during the frigid winter.

Coyote Brings Fire to the People

Long ago, the only fire in the world was on a mountaintop where three selfish Skookums lived. The Skookums were big and fearsome beings who kept fire all to themselves. Skookums did not care if humans suffered the icy fist of winter.

Coyote felt sorry for the people and decided that he would take some fire from the Skookums and bring it to the people. He made a plan and asked Squirrel, Chipmunk, and Frog to help. Late at night, the four animals went to the mountain where the Skookums lived. When the Skookums appeared to have nodded off to sleep, Coyote grabbed a flaming branch from the fire—and ran! Unfortunately, one of the Skookums was not quite asleep. The Skookums woke up and came after Coyote with menace in their eyes.

The moment Coyote felt the Skookums' touch, he shouted and tossed the fire to Squirrel. As Squirrel leapt from tree to tree, the fire scorched her back so painfully her tail curled up. She flung the fire down to Chipmunk. As the Skookums neared, Chipmunk tossed the fire to Frog. Frog caught the ember in his mouth and hopped quickly away. Before the Skookums could catch him, Frog spat the fire out onto a piece of wood. The wood swallowed the fire and it disappeared completely.

The Skookums surrounded the wood. They knew the fire was inside, but they could not get it out. They shrieked at the wood and clawed and kicked it. The wood did not give up the fire. Finally, screeching with anger, the Skookums left.

Clever Coyote knew how to get the fire out of the wood. Coyote showed the people how to rub two dry sticks together to make sparks ignite. From that time on, people knew how to get fire out of wood.

Name _____ Date _____

Use what you read in the passage to answer the questions.

1. What does the word **selfish** mean?

_____

_____

2. Where do the Skookums live?

_____

_____

3. Why does Coyote feel sorry for the people?

_____

_____

4. Who helps Coyote with his plan?

_____

_____

5. Who catches the fire after Coyote?

_____

_____

6. What causes Squirrel's tail to curl up?

_____

_____

7. Where does Frog spit the fire?

_____

_____

8. What clues help you conclude that the Skookums are upset that the fire is in the wood?

_____

_____

Brer Rabbit

One afternoon Brer Rabbit was very thirsty. He saw Sis Cow. "Sis Cow, can I have some of your milk, please?" he asked politely.

"No way," answered Sis Cow in an angry voice.

Crabby cow, Brer Rabbit said angrily to himself. But suddenly he had an idea. "Hey, Sis Cow. I want fruit in that tree." He pointed at a tall tree. "But the fruit is too high for me. Will you help? You can hit the tree with your horns so the fruit will fall."

Sis Cow agreed. She took a running start toward the tree. *Ka-pow!* She hit the tree hard. Her horns were **stuck** in the tree. She was trapped. "Help me, Brer Rabbit," Sis Cow said.

Brer Rabbit shook his head and smiled. This was Brer Rabbit's plan all along. The rabbit milked Sis Cow until the pails were full. "Good-bye for now," Brer Rabbit said. "I'll be back for more in the morning."

Sis Cow used all her strength to get out of the tree. She was angry. Sis Cow was going to give Brer Rabbit a taste of his own medicine. She pretended that she was still stuck. "Good morning," Brer Rabbit said. "I've come for more milk."

Sis Cow jumped at Brer Rabbit. Brer Rabbit hid inside a thick bush. Sis Cow called, "Brer Rabbit!" In a deep, fake voice he called out, "I am Brer Big Eyes. That rabbit ran that way."

"Thank you," said Sis Cow. She ran away.

Brer Rabbit laughed. "I fooled Sis Cow again!" he smiled.

●○○

Brer Rabbit

One afternoon Brer Rabbit was very thirsty when he saw Sis Cow grazing, or eating grass. Brer Rabbit stopped. "Sis Cow, can I have some of your milk, please?" he asked politely.

"No way," said Sis Cow rudely.

Crabby cow, Brer Rabbit muttered to himself. Suddenly Brer Rabbit had a clever idea. "Hey, Sis Cow, I can feed my family fruit in that tree. But the fruit is too high for me to reach. If you buck the tree, the fruit will fall." Sis Cow agreed and took a running start toward the tree. *Ka-pow!* She hit the tree so hard her horns were stuck in the tree.

"Help me, Brer Rabbit," Sis Cow demanded. Brer Rabbit shook his head and smiled. Getting Sis Cow stuck was Brer Rabbit's plan all along. The rabbit gathered many buckets and milked Sis Cow.

"Good-bye for now," Brer Rabbit said. "I'll be back in the morning for breakfast."

Sis Cow used all her strength to break free. "I'm free!" Sis Cow declared. "When that tricky Brer Rabbit comes, he is going to get a taste of his own medicine!" She pretended she was still stuck.

When Brer Rabbit arrived, Sis Cow pulled her horns out of the tree and lunged at Brer Rabbit. Brer Rabbit ran and hid inside a bush. Sis Cow called out, "Brer Rabbit!"

In a deep, disguised voice Brer Rabbit said, "I am Brer Big Eyes. Brer Rabbit ran that way."

"Thank you kindly," said Sis Cow as she ran off.

Brer Rabbit laughed. "I fooled Sis Cow again!" he smiled.

Brer Rabbit

One afternoon Brer Rabbit was very thirsty as he passed the field where Sis Cow grazed. Brer Rabbit stopped near Sis Cow. "Sis Cow, can I have some of your milk, please?" he asked politely.

"No," said Sis Cow sharply. "I'm not giving you my milk!"

Crabby cow, Brer Rabbit muttered to himself. Just as he was about to leave the field, an idea popped into his clever head. "Hey, Sis Cow, look up there." He pointed at a tall tree. "If you buck the tree, the persimmons will fall and I can feed my family." Sis Cow backed up and took a running start. *Ka-pow!* She hit the tree so hard her horns were stuck in it. She was trapped.

"Help me, Brer Rabbit," Sis Cow demanded. Brer Rabbit shook his head. Getting Sis Cow stuck was Brer Rabbit's plan. Brer Rabbit milked Sis Cow until many pails were full. "Good-bye for now, Sis Cow," Brer Rabbit said. "Seeing as you'll be stuck in the morning, I'll be back."

Sis Cow used all her strength to break free. It took all night, but she did it! "When that tricky Brer Rabbit comes by today, he is going to get a taste of his own medicine!" Sis Cow pretended she was still stuck.

"Good morning, Sis Cow," Brer Rabbit said. "I'm thirsty!"

Sis Cow lunged at Brer Rabbit, but Brer Rabbit scooted away. He hid inside a thick bush and poked his face through a small opening. In a deep, disguised voice Brer Rabbit called out, "I am Brer Big Eyes. Brer Rabbit ran that way."

When Sis Cow was safely away, Brer Rabbit laughed and hurried away. "I fooled Sis Cow again!" he boasted.

Name _____ Date _____

Use what you read in the passage to answer the questions.

1. Brer Rabbit asks Sis Cow for some of her <u>milk</u> .

_____

_____

2. Why does Brer Rabbit call Sis Cow crabby?

She does not want to give him her milk.

_____

3. What does Sis Cow agree to do to help Brer Rabbit get fruit from the tree?

She agreed to buck the tree to make the fruit fall.

4. What does the word **stuck** mean in this tale?

Her horns are cauht in the tree.

_____

5. Why does Brer Rabbit trick Sis Cow the first time?

He tricked her the first time because he was thirsty and she refused to give him some milk.

6. Why does Sis Cow pretend to still be stuck in the tree?

She pretened to still be stuck because he wanted to give him a tat of his own medicine

7. What does Sis Cow mean when she says she will give Brer Rabbit "a taste of his own medicine"?

She wanted to trick him like he tricked her.

_____

8. What kind of voice does Brer Rabbit use to trick Sis Cow a second time?

He used a deep (disguised) voice.

_____

Unit 5 Mini-Lesson
Pourquoi Tales

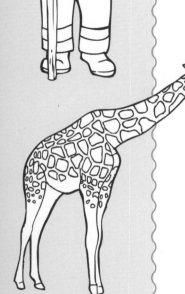

What is a pourquoi tale?

A pourquoi tale is a short story that explains why something in the natural world is the way it is. Usually the characters in a pourquoi tale are animals. Sometimes the characters are other objects in nature, such as the sun, the sky, or the sea.

What is the purpose of a pourquoi tale?

Pourquoi tales are explanations of why and how things happen in nature. These stories allow us to think about what causes the curious things we see in the world. Pourquoi tales often point out foibles, or character flaws, that people have, such as being boastful, proud, or impatient. In addition, these tales entertain us.

How do you read a pourquoi tale?

When you read a pourquoi tale, pay attention to the title. The title will help you know what question the story answers. Pay attention to the actions of the main characters as well. These actions will cause some type of change in nature. Think about how the events in the tale explain why something is the way it is.

Who invented pourquoi tales?

People have told pourquoi tales for tens of thousands of years. Many ancient cultures, including the Greeks, Chinese, and Egyptians, used these types of stories to explain nature and the universe. Many Native American, African, and Asian storytellers also used these tales to answer questions about the world.

Has a setting that is often key in the story

Is brief, with a title about something in nature

Usually has as its main characters animals or objects in nature

Pourquoi Tale

Presents a problem and a solution that explains why things in nature are a certain way

Includes a change in nature resulting from a character's actions

Has one character with a flaw

The Story of Lightning and Thunder

One winter, it snowed for a long time in the North. The people quickly packed. They went south where it was safe. In their rush to leave, the people forgot a brother and sister.

"Well, that's a pretty kettle of fish!" Brother exclaimed. He meant that this was a problem. "We are **orphans** now."

Brother and Sister looked everywhere. They could not find the people. Sister found a flint, or rock, for lighting fires. "What will we do?" she asked.

"I'll lead us to a wonderful place," said Brother. "Let me put on my sealskin boots. They will plow through snow like a knife through butter." That meant his boots would go through the snow easily.

Sister looked at the night sky. "The stars are twinkling at us. They're inviting us to live with them."

"I believe you are right!" said Brother. He kicked his boot heels together. The children floated up into the sky.

"Welcome," said one star. "You may live here if you have a magic power."

Sister said, "I can light a fire with my flint." A long scrape of the flint made a fire. It crackled and flashed brightly.

"I can make the loudest sound on Earth," answered Brother. He stomped his feet. A boom rippled across the sky. Earth shook.

"From now on, you will be called Sister Lightning and Brother Thunder," the star said.

The orphans were very, very happy. That is why Lightning and Thunder fill the sky today.

●○○

The Story of Lightning and Thunder

One winter, the snow fell hard and long in the North. The people quickly packed. They traveled south. In their haste, the villagers, or people, forgot a brother and sister.

"Well, that's a pretty kettle of fish!" Brother exclaimed. He meant that this was an odd situation. "We are orphans now."

Brother and Sister searched but could find no one. However, Sister found flint for lighting fires. "What shall we do?" she asked.

"I shall lead us to a wonderful place," said Brother. "First, let me put on my strong sealskin boots. They will plow through the snow like a knife through butter." That meant they would go through the snow very easily.

Sister looked at the night sky. "The stars are twinkling. They are inviting us to live with them."

"I believe you are right!" said Brother. He kicked his boot heels together. The two children floated up into the sky.

"You may live here if you have a magic power," said one star.

Sister said, "With my flint I can light a fire." A long scrape of the flint made a fire. It crackled and flashed brightly.

"I can make the loudest sound on Earth," said Brother. He stomped his feet. Earth shook and the stars covered their ears.

"From now on, you will be called Sister Lightning and Brother Thunder," the star said.

The orphans were ecstatic. That is why Lightning and Thunder fill the sky even to this day.

The Story of Lightning and Thunder

One winter, the snow fell hard and long in the North. The people quickly packed and set out for the south. There they would be safe and find good hunting grounds. In their haste, the villagers forgot a brother and sister.

"Well, that's a pretty kettle of fish!" Brother exclaimed. "Everyone is gone. Did our people desert us?"

Brother and Sister could find no one. However, Sister found a flint for lighting fires. "What shall we do?" she asked.

"I shall lead us to a wonderful place," said Brother. "First, let me put on my strong sealskin boots. They will plow through the snow like a knife through butter." Brother stomped through the snow.

Sister looked up at the night sky. "The stars are twinkling at us, inviting us to live with them."

"I believe you are right!" said Brother. He kicked his boot heels together and the two children floated up into the sky.

"Welcome," said one star. "You may live here if you can show me that you have a magic power."

Sister said, "With my flint I can light a fire." A long scrape of the flint produced a fire that crackled and flashed brightly.

"I can make the loudest sound on Earth," answered Brother. He stomped his feet. Earth shook and the stars covered their ears.

"You will be called Sister Lightning and Brother Thunder," the star said. The orphans were ecstatic. That is why Lightning and Thunder fill the sky even to this day.

● ● ●

Name _____ Date _____

Use what you read in the passage to answer the questions.

1. Why do the people leave the North?

_____

_____

2. Where do the people go?

_____

_____

3. What happens right after Brother says, "I believe you are right"?

_____

_____

4. How does the flint that Sister finds come in handy?

_____

_____

5. Why are Sister and Brother called **orphans**?

_____

_____

6. What is Brother's magical power?

_____

_____

7. The tale has several idioms, such as "a pretty kettle of fish." What is another idiom used in the tale?

_____

_____

8. Pourquoi tales explain things in nature. What does this tale explain?

_____

_____

Why Mosquitoes Buzz In People's Ears

Mosquito was always telling lies. He **exaggerated**. "Mosquito, you're such a pest!" Iguana yelled. He grabbed two leaves and put them into his ears. He didn't want to listen to Mosquito.

Just then Snake slithered by. "Iguana, why do you have leaves in your ears?" Snake asked. But Iguana couldn't hear a thing. "Iguana must think I'm a pest. I'll go see Rabbit."

Snake saw Rabbit's hole. He rushed in. Rabbit was having breakfast. Rabbit was surprised by Snake and ran out.

Crow was flying by. She saw Rabbit running. *Rabbits never leave their homes at breakfast time,* thought Crow. *Something bad must be happening.* "Danger! Danger!" Crow cried.

Monkey heard the warning. He slipped from a vine and landed on an owl's nest. The tiny owl fell. Mother Owl saw her baby was missing. "I will not wake the sun ever again," she promised.

The sun did not come up that day. King Lion was angry. He gathered all the animals for a meeting.

"Mother Owl, why didn't you wake up the sun?" he demanded.

Mother Owl blamed Monkey. Monkey blamed Crow for screaming "Danger! Danger!" Crow explained she was frightened when she saw Rabbit run. Rabbit said he believed Snake was going to eat him. Snake thought that Iguana was mad at him. "Oh! I put leaves in my ears because Mosquito lies all the time," said Iguana.

"Mosquito, your nonsense has got to stop," King Lion said. "From now on, you may not say another word. You may only buzz." To this day, mosquitoes' annoying stories are buzzing in people's ears.

Why Mosquitoes Buzz In People's Ears

Mosquito was a lying pest! He exaggerated all the time. Iguana had heard enough. He grabbed two leaves and put them into his ears. At that moment, Snake slithered by.

"Iguana, why do you have leaves in your ears?" Snake asked. But Iguana couldn't hear him. *Oh no,* thought Snake. *Iguana must think I'm a pest. I'll go see Rabbit.*

Snake saw Rabbit's burrow, or hole. He rushed in while Rabbit was having breakfast. Rabbit was so surprised by Snake that he ran out of his hole as fast as he could.

Crow was flying by. She saw Rabbit on the run. *Rabbits never leave their homes at breakfast time,* thought Crow. *Something bad happened.* "Danger! Danger!" Crow cried.

Monkey heard the bird's warning, fell, and landed on an owl's nest. The tiny owl fell. Mother Owl discovered her baby was missing. "I'll never hoot again nor wake the sun."

That day, the sun did not come up. King Lion was angry. "Mother Owl, why didn't you wake up the sun?" he demanded.

Mother Owl blamed Monkey for knocking her baby out of its nest. Monkey said it was Crow's fault for screaming "Danger! Danger!" Crow explained that she was frightened when she saw Rabbit run. Rabbit said he believed Snake was going to eat him. Snake thought that Iguana was mad at him. "Oh! I put leaves in my ears because of that pest, Mosquito. He's always telling me huge lies," said Iguana.

"Mosquito, your nonsense has got to stop," King Lion said. "From now on, you may not say another word. All you're allowed to do is buzz." To this day, mosquitoes' annoying stories are heard only as buzzing in people's ears.

Why Mosquitoes Buzz In People's Ears

"Stop your exaggerating! You're such a pest!" said Iguana to Mosquito. He grabbed two leaves and put them into his ears.

At that moment, Snake slithered by. "Iguana, why do you have leaves in your ears?" Snake asked. Iguana couldn't hear, so Snake thought Iguana was ignoring him. "I'll go see Rabbit."

Snake saw Rabbit's burrow and rushed in while Rabbit was having breakfast. Rabbit was so startled by Snake that he ran out of his hole as fast as he could.

Crow was flying by when she saw Rabbit on the run. *Rabbits never leave their homes at breakfast time,* thought Crow. "Danger! Danger!" Crow cried.

Monkey heard the bird's warning and slipped from a vine. He landed on an owl's nest and the tiny owl fell. Mother Owl discovered that her baby had fallen. "I'll never hoot again," she vowed. "No more will I awaken the sun each day."

That day, the sun did not come up. King Lion was angry and gathered the animals. "Mother Owl, why didn't you wake up the sun?" he demanded.

Mother Owl blamed Monkey for knocking her baby to the ground. Monkey said it was Crow's fault for screaming "Danger! Danger!" Crow explained that she was frightened when she saw Rabbit run. Rabbit said he had to flee because he believed Snake was going to eat him. Snake thought that Iguana was mad at him, so he'd gone to see Rabbit. "Oh! I put leaves in my ears because of that pest, Mosquito," said Iguana. "He's always telling me crazy stories."

"Mosquito, your nonsense has got to stop," King Lion said. "From now on, all you're allowed to do is buzz." To this day, mosquitoes can only buzz in people's ears.

Name _____ Date _____

Use what you read in the passage to answer the questions.

1. What does the word **exaggerate** mean?

_____

_____

2. What does Iguana stick in his ears? Why?

_____

_____

3. Why does Rabbit run out of his hole?

_____

_____

4. What happens after Crow sees Rabbit running?

_____

_____

5. What causes Monkey to slip?

_____

_____

6. How does Mother Owl feel? What clues help you know that?

_____

_____

7. Why is King Lion angry?

_____

_____

8. Today, mosquitoes' stories are heard only as _____.

_____

_____

Overview II: Introduction to
Informational Texts

What Is It?

What is informational text?

Nonfiction text is an important tool for learning. Informational text informs about social studies or science topics. Factual text increases our knowledge of the world.

Examples

What are some examples of informational text?

- Brochures and Pamphlets
- Encyclopedia Entries
- Magazine Articles
- Online Reference Articles
- Reference Books
- Textbooks

Purpose

What is the purpose of reading informational text?

Informational text helps us learn information as well as expands our critical thinking skills by exposing us to different thoughts and issues. It also helps prepare the brain for more difficult information as students continue schooling and prepare for real-life reading as an adult.

Audience

Who is the audience for informational text?

The audience is anyone who wants to learn something. Informational text serves to educate the reader on a topic. Some readers prefer reading nonfiction to fiction. They would rather get information they can use or that makes them smarter than read imagined stories.

How to Use It

How do you read informational text?

1. Think about what you already know about the topic.
2. Think about what you would like to know about this topic.
3. Look for vocabulary words you do not know or that seem important, such as boldfaced or repeated words.
4. Practice using reading strategies, such as monitoring comprehension.
5. After reading, note what you learned.

Overview II • Common Core Comprehension Grade 4 • ©2012 Newmark Learning, LLC

What are some common features of an informational text?

Usually includes boldfaced words or some other special text treatment to highlight words and key concepts

Includes photos or realistic drawings

Has headings and subheadings

Informational Text

Is written by someone with authentic knowledge of the topic

Is factual and backed up by research or expert opinions

May have a table of contents, glossary, index, appendix

Often has charts, graphs, maps, tables, time lines, labels, captions, and/or diagrams

Why do we study social studies?

In social studies, people learn about the people in our world and how they relate to one another. We learn how they live, manage their communities, and relate to other groups. Learning these things helps give people the intellectual skills they need to be a good citizen.

Why do we study civilizations of the Americas?

The culture, traits, and histories of the original immigrants to the Americas influenced later inhabitants and their cultures. They left behind art, stories, buildings, inventions, agriculture, and so on.

Why do we study geography?

The study of geography helps us understand the world we live in and its systems. We learn the similarities and differences between people in other lands so as to better understand our own land.

Why do we study economics?

Economics is more than just money. It is about running a business, running a government, and running your personal life. Economics studies the costs and benefits of a decision. As you get older, you will make economic decisions that will impact you, your family, and your country's economic condition.

Why do we study Native Americans?

The people who first lived in our country have a place in our history. By studying their culture and ways, we learn to appreciate their contribution to the country and their role in forming the country we have today.

Shows how peoples manage themselves and collaborate as a society

Compares peoples' similarities and differences

Encourages us to make judgments about issues

Social Studies Text

Tells about people and groups of people

Shows how governments are run

Helps teach us how to participate as a citizen in a society

Everyday Life of the Aztec

The Aztec had four classes. Classes are groups of people. The nobles were the highest class. Nobles were rich. They owned land. Some nobles lived in palaces. The commoners were the second-highest class. Most people were commoners. Farmers and workers were commoners. The third class was the serfs. Serfs worked on land owned by nobles. Slaves were the lowest class. Some slaves were captured in war. Other slaves had committed crimes.

School was important to the Aztec. One kind of school taught boys how to farm and be soldiers. Girls learned how to cook food and raise children. There were also temple schools. Boys learned to be priests or leaders at temple schools. Nobles went to the temple schools.

The Aztec had many gods and goddesses. The Aztec believed their gods ruled **agriculture**. Agriculture is farming. The Aztec wanted to make the gods happy. They thought if the gods were happy, crops would grow well.

The Aztec believed their gods needed blood to be strong. The priests gave the gods human blood. They did this by killing slaves. They also killed people captured in wars.

Most Aztec were farmers. Corn was the most important crop. The Aztec also grew beans and squash.

Tenochtitlán was the capital city. It had a large market. More than 60,000 people went to the market each day. The Aztec did not use money. They traded, or swapped, goods. They traded food, feathers, animal skins, and beans.

Everyday Life of the Aztec

The Aztec had four classes, or groups, of people. The highest class was the nobles. Nobles were rich. They owned land. Some nobles lived in palaces. The second-highest class was the commoners. Most people were commoners. They were farmers and workers. The third class was the serfs. Serfs worked on land owned by nobles. The lowest class was the slaves. Some slaves were people captured in war. Other slaves were people who had broken the law. They had committed crimes.

Education was important to the Aztec. The Aztec had different schools. In one kind of school, boys learned how to farm and be soldiers. Girls learned how to cook and raise children. Another kind of school was a temple school. At temple schools, boys learned to be priests or leaders. Nobles went to the temple schools.

The Aztec had many gods and goddesses. They thought their gods ruled agriculture, or farming. The Aztec tried to please the gods so that they could grow good crops.

The Aztec believed that blood kept their gods strong. The priests offered human blood by making sacrifices. They killed slaves or people captured in wars. The Aztec believed the souls of these people would go to a special place.

Most Aztec were farmers, and corn was the most important crop. The Aztec also grew beans and squash.

Tenochtitlán had a large market. People went to the market to trade. More than 60,000 people went to the market each day. The Aztec did not use money. They traded goods. They traded food, feathers, animal skins, beans, and special stones.

Everyday Life of the Aztec

Aztec people were separated into classes, or types. The highest class was nobles. They had high social rank, or position. The second-highest class was commoners. Commoners were ordinary people. Most of the people were commoners.

The third class was made up of serfs. Serfs worked on land held by nobles. The lowest class was slaves. They were thought of as property. Slaves were people who had been captured in war or had committed a crime. Some had not paid a debt they owed.

Education was very important to the Aztec. There were two kinds of schools. In one school, children studied history and religion. Boys learned how to farm and become soldiers. Girls were taught how to raise a family and make a good home. The other kind of school was run by a temple. Temple schools taught boys to be priests or other types of leaders. Nobles often went to temple schools.

The Aztec believed that gods and goddesses ruled agriculture, or farming. The Aztec thought it was important to please the gods in order to grow good crops. They also believed that human hearts and blood kept their gods strong. So they made human sacrifices. Most of the people sacrificed were slaves or prisoners taken in war. The Aztec believed the souls of the people sacrificed would go to a special place.

Most of the Aztec were farmers, and corn was the most important crop. They also farmed beans and squash.

Tenochtitlán had the largest market in the Americas. People went there to trade crops and other things. More than 60,000 people went to this market every day. The Aztec did not use money. They traded things with one another. They traded feathers, animal skins, beans, and rubber.

Name _____ Date _____

Use what you read in the passage to answer the questions.

1. What was the Aztec's highest class?

_____

_____

2. What class were most people?

_____

_____

3. How were the two kinds of Aztec schools different?

_____

_____

4. Which class went to temple schools?

_____

_____

5. What is **agriculture**?

_____

_____

6. What crops did the Aztec grow?

_____

_____

7. What did people do at the market in Tenochtitlán?

_____

_____

8. What conclusions can you draw about war from the passage?

_____

_____

The Northeast

The Northeast has many types of landforms. Landforms are mountains, rivers, lakes, and seacoasts. The Northeast has snowy mountains. The Northeast has sandy beaches, too.

The Appalachian Mountains are in the Northeast. They are in Canada and the United States. They are ancient, or very old, mountains. They have eroded over millions of years. *Eroded* means "worn down."

East of the mountains is the Atlantic coastal plain. It is called Atlantic because of the Atlantic Ocean. A coastal plain is a long, flat stretch of land. A coastal plain is on a seacoast. A coastal plain has beaches, wetlands, and barrier islands. Barrier islands are long and thin. They help keep the seacoast safe. The islands act like a wall. They stop the beaches on the coast from washing away.

A cape is a part of a coast that sticks out into the sea. Cape Cod is in Massachusetts. It has water on three sides. Many people go to Cape Cod on hot summer days. Cape Cod is known for its great beaches. It is also a good place to fish.

The Northeast has many rivers and lakes. Two famous lakes are Lake Erie and Lake Ontario. Both lakes are Great Lakes. The Great Lakes form a border between Canada and New York. The Great Lakes are the largest freshwater lakes in the world. The water in a freshwater lake is not salty. Rivers often connect two lakes. The Niagara River joins Lake Erie and Lake Ontario. The river is not very long. It has one very special feature: a tall, wide waterfall. The river flows over a 170-foot cliff.

The Northeast

The Northeast has many types of landforms. Landforms are mountains, rivers, lakes, and seacoasts. You can find snowy mountains in the Northeast. You can find sandy beaches there, too.

The Appalachian Mountains run through most of the Northeast. They go from Canada to Alabama. They are ancient mountains. They have eroded, or worn down, over millions of years.

East of the mountains you see the Atlantic coastal plain. Atlantic stands for the Atlantic Ocean. A coastal plain is a long, flat stretch of land. A coastal plain runs along a seacoast. A coastal plain has beaches, wetlands, and barrier islands. Barrier islands are long and thin. They help keep the seacoast safe. The islands act like a wall. This stops the beaches on the coast from eroding, or washing away.

A cape is a part of a coast that sticks out into the sea. Cape Cod is in Massachusetts. It has water on three sides. On hot summer days, many people go to Cape Cod. Cape Cod is known for its great beaches. It is also a good place to fish.

The Northeast has many rivers and lakes. Two famous lakes are Lake Erie and Lake Ontario. These two lakes are part of the Great Lakes. The Great Lakes form a border between Canada and New York. The Great Lakes are the largest freshwater lakes in the world. The water in a freshwater lake is not salty. Rivers often join lakes. The Niagara River joins Lake Erie and Lake Ontario. The river is not very long. It has one very special feature, though. It has a tall, wide waterfall. The river flows over a 170-foot cliff.

The Northeast

The Northeast has many kinds of landforms, such as mountains and valleys. It also has rivers, lakes, and seacoasts. The Northeast has it all—from snow-covered mountain peaks to hot, sandy beaches.

The Appalachian Mountains run through most of the Northeast. They start in Canada and end in Alabama. Because the Appalachians are ancient mountains, they have eroded, or worn down, over millions of years. Look east of the Appalachian Mountains and you'll see the Atlantic coastal plain. It's the long, flat stretch of land that runs along the seacoast. Here you'll see beaches, barrier islands, and wetlands. Barrier islands are long, narrow, sandy beaches that run parallel to the shore. They stop storms and tides from washing away the beaches on the coast.

On a warm, sunny day in summer, Cape Cod, Massachusetts, is a great place to be. It is known for its beautiful beaches and fine fishing. A cape is a piece of the coast that sticks out into the sea. Cape Cod is a narrow, hook-shaped piece of land. It has water on three sides.

Many states in the Northeast border the Atlantic Ocean. In addition, the region has many rivers and lakes you can enjoy. The Great Lakes are some of the biggest freshwater lakes in the world. They form a water border between New York and Canada. There are five Great Lakes. The two smallest lakes, Erie and Ontario, are in the Northeast. The Niagara River connects Lake Erie and Lake Ontario. Along its short path, the river plunges over cliffs about 170 feet (52 meters) high, creating Niagara Falls, a waterfall.

Name _____ Date _____

Use what you read in the passage to answer the questions.

1. What kinds of landforms are in the Northeast?

_____

_____

2. What happened to the Appalachian Mountains over time?

_____

_____

3. The Appalachian Mountains are in which country or countries?

_____

_____

4. How do barrier islands keep beaches from washing away?

_____

_____

5. Why might people visit Cape Cod in the summer?

_____

_____

6. Which of the Great Lakes are in the Northeast?

_____

_____

7. What makes the Niagara River unique, or special?

_____

_____

8. What ocean is near the Northeast states?

_____

_____

Athens: The Glory of Greece

Ancient Greece was made up of **city-states**. A city-state included the main city and the area around it. Athens was one famous city-state. We call the people of Athens the Athenians.

The Athenians came up with the idea of democracy. A democracy is a government ruled by the people. Athenian men gathered to vote several times a month.

In ancient Greece, the outdoor market was called the agora. The agora was the center of commerce. Commerce means trading food and goods.

Most people in Athens were farmers. But Greek soil was thin. It didn't always rain when the farmers needed it to. For these reasons, farming in Greece was hard. The Greeks did grow olives, grapes, and figs. The Greeks also grew vegetables, fruits, and herbs. The main food they ate was bread. But the Greek farmers could not grow enough grain to feed themselves. So they traded with other countries for grain.

One of Athens's main exports was silver. An export is something you sell to or trade with another country. The Athenians made silver into coins. Their famous coins had the Athenian owl on one side. The owl was the symbol of the goddess Athena.

The economic system in Athens depended on farming. Slave workers were needed to farm. Slaves also worked in homes and in the silver mines.

Athens had a strong economy. The Athenians' great literature, art, and ideas still influence the world today. Their democracy has been a model for many modern free nations.

Athens: The Glory of Greece

The civilization of ancient Greece was made up of city-states. A city-state had a main city and included the territory around it. One famous city-state was Athens. We call the people of Athens the Athenians.

The Athenians developed the first form of democracy. A democracy is a government ruled by the people. Their democracy required the male citizens of Athens to vote several times a month in an assembly called the *ekklesia*.

In ancient Greece, the agora was an open-air market. The agora was the center of daily life and commerce. These markets were where people traded food and goods. In addition to trading goods, people also shared news at the agora.

Most people in Athens were farmers. Only citizens were allowed to own land. But Greek soil was thin. People could not depend on the rain. For these reasons, farming in Greece was hard. The Greeks did grow olives, grapes, and figs. The Greeks also grew vegetables, fruits, and herbs. But the main food of their diet was bread. They could not grow enough grain to feed themselves. So the Greeks traded with other countries for grain.

One of Athens's main exports was silver. The Athenians minted the silver into coins. Their famous coins showed the Athenian owl on one side. The owl symbolized the goddess Athena. The value of the coin was equal to the value of the silver in the coin.

Athens had a strong economy. Its great literature, art, and ideas still influence the world today. Their democracy has been a model for many modern free nations.

Athens: The Glory of Greece

The civilization of ancient Greece was made up of city-states. A city-state consisted of an independent city and the territory around it. One famous city-state was Athens. The Athenians developed the first form of democracy. This government by the people required the male citizens of Athens to vote several times a month in an assembly called the *ekklesia*.

In ancient Greece, the agora, or open-air marketplace, was the center of daily life and commerce. These markets, where people traded food and goods, were located in the middle of each city. In addition to trading goods, people also shared information at the agora. They gossiped, discussed philosophy, and debated about whom to vote for in the next election.

The Athenians were mainly farmers. They put a high value on owning land, which only citizens were allowed to have. But Greek soil was thin and rain was unreliable. For these reasons, farming in Greece was hard. The Greeks did grow some important crops, such as olives, grapes, and figs. These crops grew well in the Mediterranean climate. The Greeks also grew vegetables, fruits, and herbs, including cabbages and pomegranates. But the main food of their diet was bread.

One of Athens's main exports was silver. An export is something you sell to or trade with another country. The Athenians made silver into coins. Their famous coins had the Athenian owl on one side. The owl was the symbol of the goddess Athena.

The Athenian economic system, along with their democratic government and independent spirit, allowed Athenians to flourish. Their great literature, art, and ideas still influence the world today. Their democracy has been a model for many modern free nations.

Name _____ Date _____

Use what you read in the passage to answer the questions.

1. What civilization is this passage about?

_____

_____

2. What are **city-states**?

_____

_____

3. What clues support the conclusion that the goddess Athena was important to the ancient Greeks?

_____

_____

4. What was an agora?

_____

_____

5. Why was farming hard in ancient Greece?

_____

_____

6. What was the ancient Greeks' main food?

_____

_____

7. What kind of government did the Athenians have?

_____

_____

8. How does ancient Athens influence the world today?

_____

_____

Traditional Ways of Life

In the early 1700s, southwest Indian tribes brought horses to the Plains. Plains are flat land covered in grass with few trees. They are in the Midwest of the United States. The people living in the Plains had never seen horses. The Plains people learned to ride. Hunters followed the herds. The horses helped them hunt more easily.

With horses, many Plains tribes hunted buffalo all year. The Plains Indians used almost every part of a buffalo. Women used the meat to make stews. They made tepees and clothes from the skins. They made tools and sleds from the bones. The people were able to get almost everything they needed to live from the buffalo.

The Comanche were a tribe. They lived on the southern plains. They became great horseback riders. They were also good hunters. Boys and girls began riding when they were very young.

The Comanche hunted in groups. The groups were called **bands**. Over time, bands formed larger groups. They were called divisions. Divisions were named for favorite Comanche foods. One was called the Root Eaters. The Buffalo Eaters was another group.

The Comanche were **nomads**. Nomads are people who wander. They don't stay in one place. Other tribes, like the Hidatsa, stayed in one place. The Hidatsa lived in the northern plains.

The Plains Indians focused on family. Mothers and fathers took care of their children. Other family members took care of the children, too. A grandfather might take a boy on his first hunting trip. An aunt might teach a girl how to prepare a buffalo skin. Games and chores prepared children for life.

Traditional Ways of Life

In the early 1700s, southwest Indian tribes brought horses to the Plains. The Plains people had never seen horses before. They called them "mystery dogs." The Plains people learned to ride. Hunters followed the herds. They could hunt more easily.

With horses, many Plains tribes began to hunt animals like buffalo all year. The Plains Indians used almost every part of a buffalo. Women used the meat to make stews. They made the skins into tepees and clothes. They made bones into tools and sleds. The buffalo gave the people almost all they needed.

The Comanche were one tribe. This tribe lived on the southern plains. They became great horseback riders. They were also good hunters. Boys and girls began riding at a very young age. Most boys had their own horse at age five.

Comanche men and other tribes hunted in groups called bands. Over time, bands formed larger groups called divisions. These divisions were named for favorite Comanche foods. One was called the Root Eaters. The Buffalo Eaters was the name of another group.

The Comanche were nomads. Other tribes, like the Hidatsa, stayed in one place. This tribe lived in villages near rivers on the northern plains.

The Plains Indians had strong family ties. Mothers and fathers cared for their children. So did other family members. A grandfather might take a boy on his first hunting trip. An aunt might teach a girl how to prepare a buffalo skin. Games and chores prepared children for the future.

Traditional Ways of Life

Before the 1700s, most Plains Indian tribes lived in villages near rivers. They fished and grew vegetables. A few men hunted buffalo. Hunting was difficult because the Indians did not have horses yet.

The Plains Indians got horses from southwest Indian tribes in the early 1700s. The Plains people had never seen horses before. They called them "mystery dogs." But they quickly learned to ride.

Once they had horses, many Plains tribes decided to hunt all year. They became nomads. The Plains Indians used almost every part of a buffalo. Women cooked stews with the meat. They made the buffalo skins into tepee covers and clothing. Bones made good tools and sleds.

The Comanche were one Plains Indian tribe. Comanche men hunted in groups called bands. Over time, they formed larger groups called divisions. The divisions became known by the names of the Comanche's favorite foods. One was called the Root Eaters. The Buffalo Eaters was another group.

While the Comanche were nomads, other tribes, such as the Hidatsa, stayed in one place.

The Plains Indians had strong family ties. Mothers and fathers cared for their children. Brothers and sisters often played together. They did many of the same activities as the adults. They set up tepees. Boys pretended to hunt buffalo. Girls sewed robes. Games and chores prepared children for the future.

Name _____ Date _____

Use what you read in the passage to answer the questions.

1. What did southwest Indian tribes bring to the Plains Indians in the 1700s?

_____

_____

2. How did horses make it easier to hunt?

_____

_____

3. In what ways did the Plains Indians come to depend on buffalo?

_____

_____

4. What does the word **bands** mean in this passage?

_____

_____

5. What is one of the Comanche's favorite foods?

_____

_____

6. What are **nomads**?

_____

_____

7. How did the Plains Indians prepare children for the future?

_____

_____

8. How is your family similar to or different from Plains Indian families?

_____

_____

Science

Why do we study science?

Science helps us understand the world around us. To participate in society, one must know some science. As examples, to cook dinner you must understand hot and cold, chemical reactions, and the effects of combinations of ingredients. When you choose to eat an apple rather than a bag of chips, you have considered your nutrition. These decisions involve science understanding.

Why do we study life science?

Earth is full of life, and life science studies the living things on Earth. Life science studies animals and plants and the environments and habitats in which they live. It studies how living things meet their needs for water and food. And it studies the life cycles of living things—how they grow and change over time.

Why do we study earth science?

Earth science is the study of Earth as well as things in outer space. Builders use earth science to protect their buildings against high winds and earthquakes. Since we all live on Earth, we all must make decisions to prevent pollution, use energy responsibly, ration resources, and be a caretaker of our planet.

Why do we study physical science?

Physical science involves the study of nonliving things in our world. When you use a fan to cool you off, or when you use a magnet to pick up a tack, you are employing physical science. Physical science study in school often includes laboratory work, such as experiments.

Contains factual information about our planet and its neighbors in space

Studies how life forms change over time

Shows how different plants and animals live

Tells about the differences in living and nonliving things

Inspires us to think like scientists

Science Text

Includes special text features, such as photos, labels, captions, diagrams, and sidebars

Explains scientific terms

Encourages good decisions about protecting and preserving the environment

Plants

How are plants different from other living things? Plants were one of the first living things. Plants have been on Earth for millions of years. More than 400,000 kinds of plants grow on Earth. All living things are made of cells. The cell is a basic and tiny part of all living things. Plants are made of cells. Animals are made of cells, too. You are made of cells.

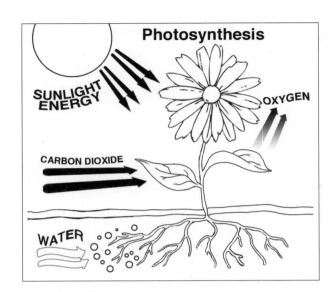

Plant cells and animal cells are alike in some ways. All cells are about sixty percent water. Different cell parts float in this water. All cells have a nucleus. The nucleus tells the cell what to do. Plant and animal cells are different in some ways. All plant cells have a cell wall. Animal cells do not have a cell wall. A cell wall gives a plant its shape. Cell walls also hold a plant straight up. Being straight up protects plants from wind, rain, and snow. Plant cells have chloroplasts. Chloroplasts have chlorophyll. Chlorophyll is the green in plants. Animal cells do not have chloroplasts. Chlorophyll uses light to make food. Plants make food by photosynthesis. *Photo* means "light." *Synthesis* means "to mix."

Plants need water and light to make food. They also need gas. The gas is **carbon dioxide**. Plant roots take in water. Plant leaves take in carbon dioxide. Plant leaves get light from the sun. The chloroplast uses sunlight to mix the water and gas. Then the chloroplast makes sugar. Plants use sugar as food. Plants also make oxygen. Oxygen is a gas in the air. People and animals help plants. We give them carbon dioxide. Plants give us oxygen to breathe. This is one way that plants and animals keep Earth in balance.

Plants

Have you ever wondered what makes plants different from other living things? Plants were one of the first types of living things. Plants have been on Earth for millions of years. More than 400,000 types of plants grow on Earth. All living things are made of cells. The cell is the basic building block of living things. Plants and animals are made of cells. You are made of cells, too.

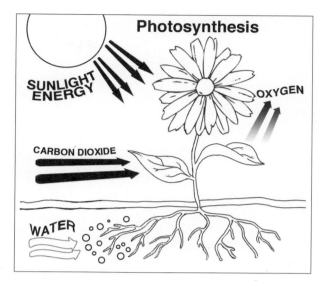

Plant cells and animal cells are alike in some ways. All cells are about sixty percent water. Different cell parts float in this water. All cells have a nucleus. The nucleus tells the cell what to do. Plant and animal cells are different in some ways, too. All plant cells have a cell wall. Animal cells do not have a cell wall. Cell walls give a plant its shape. Cell walls also hold a plant straight up. This helps plants stay healthy in wind, rain, and snow. Plant cells have chloroplasts. Animal cells do not have chloroplasts. Chloroplasts hold chlorophyll. Chlorophyll gives a plant its green color. Chlorophyll helps plants use light to make food. Plants make food by photosynthesis. *Photo* means "light." *Synthesis* means "to mix."

Plants need water, light, and a gas to make food. The gas is carbon dioxide. Plant roots take in water. Plant leaves take in carbon dioxide. Plant leaves get light from the sun. Sunlight helps the chloroplast mix the water and gas. Then the chloroplast makes sugar. Plants use sugar as food. This process makes oxygen. Plants let oxygen out into the air. People and animals help plants. We give them carbon dioxide. Plants give us oxygen to breathe. This is one way that plants and animals keep Earth in balance.

Plants

Plants have been on Earth for hundreds of millions of years. More than 400,000 types of plants grow on Earth. Plants, animals, and humans are all made of cells. All cells are about sixty percent water. The water and carbon compounds make up the semi-fluid portion of a cell, the cytoplasm. The parts of a cell are called organelles. Each plant cell has a cell wall. The cell walls give a plant its shape. The cell walls also hold a plant upright. This is important because plants need to withstand pressure from wind, rain, and snow. The nucleus is an organelle near the center of a cell. The nucleus carries all the information needed to make a new cell. It tells a cell when and how to get food, to make energy, and to make a new plant.

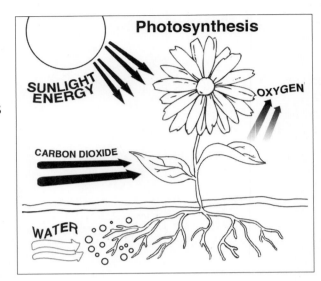

Plant cells have special parts that are not found in the cells of any other organism. The special organelles are called chloroplasts. Chloroplasts contain chlorophyll. Chlorophyll is the chemical that gives a plant its green color. Chlorophyll reacts with light to allow a plant to make its own food. Plants make food through a complex series of events. Together, these events are called photosynthesis, which means "to mix with light."

Plants absorb a gas called carbon dioxide through tiny holes in their leaves. They take in water through roots in the soil. Sunlight causes chlorophyll to react with the water and carbon dioxide. The result is a kind of sugar that the plant uses for food. People and animals help plants by supplying them with carbon dioxide. Plants help animals and people by replacing the oxygen in the air we breathe. This cycle is just one way that plants and animals coexist.

Name _____ Date _____

Use what you read in the passage to answer the questions.

1. What were among the first living things on Earth?

_____

_____

2. How many kinds of plants grow on Earth?

_____

_____

3. How are you and a plant alike?

_____

_____

4. Why is the nucleus an important part of the cell?

_____

_____

5. What role does the cell wall have in a plant's survival?

_____

_____

6. What gives a plant its green color?

_____

_____

7. What is **carbon dioxide**?

_____

_____

8. How do plants and animals (including people) help one another?

_____

_____

Kingdoms to Species

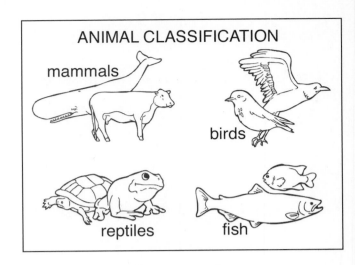

ANIMAL CLASSIFICATION

mammals

birds

reptiles

fish

Scientists sort animals into groups. A kingdom is the largest group of living things. All plants are in the plant kingdom. All animals are in the animal kingdom. There are five kingdoms. Kingdoms have smaller groups. Those groups are called phyla. The animal kingdom has three main phyla. One phylum is arthropods. Arthropods have exoskeletons. Exoskeletons are skeletons on the outside of a body. Most insects are arthropods.

Another phylum is chordates. Chordates are animals with a spinal cord. A spinal cord is nerve tissue that takes messages from the brain to the rest of the body. In some animals, the spinal cord is wrapped in bone. The spinal cord and bone form a backbone. Chordates with backbones are vertebrates. Chordates that do not have backbones are invertebrates. Each phylum has smaller groups. They are called classes. All birds are in the same class. Animals that feed milk to their young are another class. This class is mammals. Classes have smaller groups. They are called orders. Primates are one order. Primates are animals with obvious hands and feet.

Orders have smaller groups called families. The primate order has a family called Hominidae. The Hominidae family includes humans, gorillas, and chimpanzees. Genus is the next-smallest group. Foxes, wolves, and dogs belong to the same family. But only wolves and dogs are in the same genus. Species is the smallest group of all. A collie, a poodle, and a German shepherd are all dogs. They are all in the same species.

Kingdoms to Species

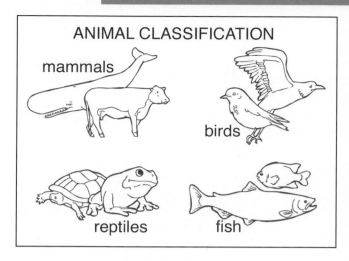

ANIMAL CLASSIFICATION
mammals
birds
reptiles
fish

Scientists sort animals into groups based on shared traits. Kingdoms are the largest groups of living things. All plants are in the plant kingdom. All animals are in the animal kingdom. There are five kingdoms in all. Kingdoms have smaller groups called phyla. The animal kingdom has three main phyla. One phylum is arthropods. Another phylum of animals is chordates. Arthropods have hard skeletons outside their bodies. These skeletons are exoskeletons. Most insects are arthropods.

Chordates are animals that have a spinal cord. The spinal cord of some chordates is wrapped in bone. The spinal cord and bone form a backbone. Chordates with backbones are vertebrates. A few chordates do not have backbones. These chordates are invertebrates.

Each phylum has smaller groups called classes. All birds are in the same class. Birds have feathers. Animals that feed milk to their young are in another class. This class is mammals. Humans are mammals. Orders come after classes. Primates are one order. Primates are animals with obvious hands and feet.

Orders have smaller groups called families. For example, the primate order has a family called Hominidae. This family includes humans, gorillas, and chimpanzees. Genus is the next-smallest group. Foxes, wolves, and dogs belong to the same family. Only wolves and dogs are in the same genus. Species is the smallest group of all. A collie, a poodle, and a German shepherd are all dogs. They are all in the same species.

Kingdoms to Species

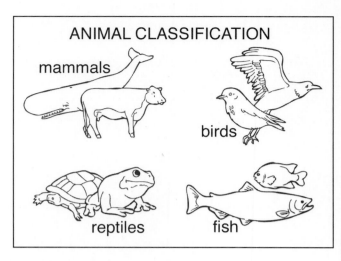

ANIMAL CLASSIFICATION

mammals

birds

reptiles

fish

Classification is the process of putting things in groups. All organisms are grouped by similar characteristics, or traits. The kingdom is the largest group of organisms. A kingdom includes all organisms that are alike in some major way. For instance, the animal kingdom includes just animals, and the plant kingdom includes just plants. There are five kingdoms in all. Kingdoms are next divided into phyla. The two largest phyla are arthropods and chordates. Arthropods are animals that do not have a spinal cord or an internal skeleton like humans. They have an exoskeleton, or external skeleton. An exoskeleton is like a shell. Most insects are arthropods. Chordates have a spinal cord. The spinal cord is a fiber of nerves that runs along the backs of chordates. Chordates that have a spinal cord encased in bone are vertebrates. Chordates that don't are invertebrates.

As animals are organized into smaller groups, the animals become more alike. For example, birds are grouped together in a class because they have feathers. Animals that feed milk to their young are another class—mammals. Humans are mammals. Once they are organized in classes, all organisms are then placed in orders. The order of primates includes animals that have well-developed hands and feet, a short nose, and a large brain. Orders are divided into smaller groups called families. For example, the primate order contains a family called Hominidae. Hominidae includes humans, chimpanzees, and gorillas. Genus and species are the final two groups in the classification system. Foxes, wolves, and dogs belong to the same family. However, foxes are in a different genus than wolves and dogs. A collie, a poodle, and a German shepherd are all dogs. They are all in the same species.

Name _____ Date _____

Use what you read in the passage to answer the questions.

1. What system is used to sort animals?

_____

_____

2. What is the name of the largest group?

_____

_____

3. Where is an arthropod's skeleton?

_____

_____

4. Which phyla are most insects in?

_____

_____

5. What do all chordates have?

_____

_____

6. How are a vertebrate and an invertebrate different?

_____

_____

7. All birds are in the same _____.

_____

_____

8. What's the group before genus?

_____

_____

Earthquakes

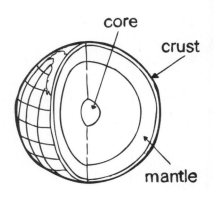

The year was 1906. Most people in San Francisco were still asleep. Suddenly an earthquake hit the city. An earthquake is when the ground shakes hard. Many buildings fell. Thousands of people died. There were fires. The city burned for days.

Earth has many layers. The outer layer is the crust. The crust is the ground you stand on. The crust is broken up into huge pieces. The pieces are called plates. The plates move all the time. The plates float on a part of Earth called the mantle. Look at the diagram to see the layers.

The crust has many cracks, or breaks, in it. These cracks are called **faults**. Sometimes rocks get stuck in a fault. The plates push hard against the rocks. Sometimes the rocks break. When that happens, the plates move suddenly. This makes Earth's crust shake. This is an earthquake. Scientists watch the large faults carefully. Earthquakes are likely to happen in these same faults.

There were three very big earthquakes in 1811 and 1812. The earthquakes happened near New Madrid, Missouri. Many things happened to the land because of the earthquakes. Large areas sank. New lakes formed. Forests were destroyed. One earthquake even changed the path of the Mississippi River!

December 26, 2004, began as a quiet morning in South Asia. Then an earthquake hit. It hit deep in the Indian Ocean. The earthquake caused a tsunami. A tsunami is a giant wave. The tsunami moved quickly across the Indian Ocean. The people in South Asia had no warning about the tsunami. Suddenly, they saw the ocean do something strange. It pulled back suddenly. People could see the bottom of the ocean. Then a wall of water slammed onto the beach. More than 200,000 people died. Scientists are working hard to find a way to warn people next time.

Earthquakes

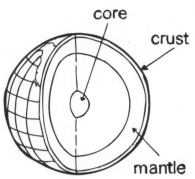

core

crust

mantle

It was early on an April morning in 1906. Most people in San Francisco were still asleep. Then a terrible earthquake hit the city. Many buildings fell. Thousands of people died. The city burned for days.

Earth has many layers. The outer layer is the crust. The crust is the ground you are standing on. It is also the floor of the ocean. The crust is broken up into huge pieces. The pieces are called plates. These plates move all the time. They float on the mantle. Look at the diagram to see the layers.

The crust has many cracks in it. These cracks are called faults. Sometimes rocks get stuck along a fault. The plates push hard against the rocks. If the rocks break, the plates move suddenly. This makes Earth's crust start to shake. This is an earthquake. Scientists watch the large faults carefully. Earthquakes are likely to happen there again.

In 1811 and 1812, three very big earthquakes struck near New Madrid, Missouri. They made big changes to the land. Large areas of land sank. New lakes formed. Forests were destroyed. One quake even changed the path of the Mississippi River!

The date was December 26, 2004. It was a quiet morning in South Asia. Then an earthquake hit. It struck deep in the Indian Ocean. The quake caused a tsunami, or giant wave. The tsunami spread across the Indian Ocean. Its speed was 500 miles (805 kilometers) per hour! The wave slowed as it reached the shore. The people in South Asia had no warning. They saw the ocean do a strange thing. It pulled back suddenly. People could see the ocean floor. Then a wall of water slammed onto the beach. More than 200,000 people died. Scientists are working on a warning system.

Earthquakes

It was 5:12 A.M. on an April morning in
1906. Most people were still asleep when
San Francisco was hit by one of the worst
earthquakes on record. In less than one minute,
the ground moved more than twenty feet.
Dozens of buildings were flattened. Thousands lost
their lives. The city burned for days following the earthquake.

Earth has four major layers. The outer layer is the crust. It
includes the ground and the ocean floor. The crust is broken
up into huge pieces called plates. These plates move all the
time, floating on the mantle.

The crust has many cracks called faults. When rocks
get stuck along a fault, the plates keep moving. The plates
push hard against the rocks. If the rocks break, the plates
move suddenly and Earth's crust starts to shake. This is an
earthquake. Earthquakes also happen when one plate sinks
under another one, or when plates crash or grind past each
other. Earthquakes are likely to happen in these areas again.

In 1811 and 1812, three very big earthquakes struck near
New Madrid, Missouri. They changed Earth's surface more than
any other earthquake in North America. Large areas of land
sank, new lakes formed, and acres of forests were destroyed.
One quake even changed the course of the Mississippi River!

The morning of December 26, 2004, started out peacefully
in South Asia. Then a huge earthquake struck deep in the
Indian Ocean. The quake caused a tsunami, or giant wave.
The tsunami spread across the Indian Ocean at speeds of
500 miles (805 kilometers) per hour! As it reached the shore,
it slowed. The first wave was 30 feet (9.1 meters) tall when
it crashed on shore. People along the Indian Ocean had no
warning. Right before the big wave hit, the ocean suddenly
pulled back. People could see the ocean floor. Then a wall
of water slammed onto the coast. More than 200,000 people
died. Scientists are working to make better warning systems.

Name _____ Date _____

Use what you read in the passage to answer the questions.

1. What were the effects of the 1906 earthquake in San Francisco?

_____

_____

2. What is the outer layer of Earth called?

_____

_____

3. What are **faults**?

_____

_____

4. What can you infer causes the rocks in the faults to break?

_____

_____

5. Why do scientists watch the larger faults carefully?

_____

_____

6. In what years did big earthquakes hit New Madrid, Missouri?

_____

_____

7. What caused the tsunami to form on December 26, 2004, in South Asia?

_____

_____

8. Why were the people of South Asia not prepared for the tsunami?

_____

_____

It Matters

It's lunchtime. You eat a sandwich and soup. Then you start to think, *What is the sandwich made of? What is the soup made of? What is the air made of?* They are all made of **matter**. Matter is anything that takes up space and has mass. Everything on Earth is made of matter. You're made of matter, too.

Matter has three different states. A state is a form of something. The states of matter are solids, liquids, and gases. Each state of matter has properties. Properties tell us how something looks. They tell us how something feels or smells.

Most things you can see are solids. A book is a solid. A chair is a solid. The window is a solid. Solids have a shape. Solids stay the same shape when you hold them. Pick up a book. The book keeps its shape.

Water is matter, too. But water is a liquid. A liquid needs to be in something. Whatever it's in is the shape a liquid takes. Think of water in a glass. The water takes the shape of the glass. A liquid is different from a solid in another way. We can pour a liquid. It flows.

Think of a cup of hot cocoa. The cocoa is a liquid. The cup is a solid. The steam coming from the hot cocoa is another state of matter. It is a gas. A gas has no shape. Gas fills the space it is in. How do we know that gas takes up space? Blow up a balloon. It is empty until you blow into it. It fills up with air. Air is a gas.

All matter is made up of elements. Elements are basic types of matter. Gold is an element. Iron is an element, too.

It Matters

It's lunchtime. You eat a sandwich and sip soup. You take a deep breath. Then you start to think, *What is the sandwich made of? What is the soup made of? What is the air made of?* They are all made of matter. Matter is anything that takes up space and has mass. Everything on Earth is made of matter. That means you, too.

Not all matter is the same. Matter has three different states, or forms. The states are solids, liquids, and gases. Each state of matter has certain properties. Properties tell us how something looks. Properties also tell us how something feels or smells.

Look around. Most things you can see are solids. Solids have a definite shape. They keep their shape when you hold them. Pick up a book. The book keeps its shape. Put the book down. It stays in place. Water is a different type of matter. Water is a liquid. A liquid needs something to hold it. The holder gives it a shape. Think of water in a glass. The water takes on the shape of the glass. A liquid is different from a solid in another way. A liquid can be poured. It flows.

Think of a cup of hot cocoa. The hot cocoa is a liquid. The cup is a solid. What is the steam rising from the cup? The steam is another type of matter. It is a gas. A gas has no shape. Gas fills whatever space it is in. Does gas take up space? Take an empty balloon. Blow air into it. The balloon fills up with air. The air is a gas. So gas takes up space.

All matter is made up of elements. Elements are basic types of matter. Gold is an element. Iron is an element, too.

It Matters

It's a lovely day to eat outside. You eat your sandwich and sip soup as the air touches your face. Then you wonder what the sandwich, the soup, and the air have in common. They are all made of matter. Matter is anything that takes up space and has mass. Everything on Earth is made of matter—even you. There are three different forms, or states, of matter. They are solids, liquids, and gases. Each state of matter has certain characteristics. Properties describe how an object looks, feels, and behaves.

Most things you see are solids. Solids have a definite shape. The shape stays the same when you hold or move a solid. Pick up a pencil and hold it. It keeps its shape. Put the pencil down and it still has the same shape.

Orange juice and water are liquids. A liquid needs a container to hold it and give it a shape. A liquid is different from a solid in another way. A liquid flows, which means it can be poured. Hot cocoa is also a liquid. The cup it is in is a solid. The air around the cup is a gas. A gas has no shape. It fills whatever space it is in. What about the steam rising from the hot cocoa? That is also a gas.

How do we know that gas takes up space? A balloon is an empty bag until you blow into it. It fills up with air, which is a gas. All matter is made up of elements. Elements are basic kinds of matter found in nature. The gold in a ring is an element. Iron is an element. The oxygen in the air is an element. Scientists have learned that elements are made of atoms. Atoms are the smallest pieces, or particles, of any element. Atoms of elements join together to form compounds. Salt and water are compounds. Many compounds are made up of small units called molecules.

Name _____ Date _____

Use what you read in the passage to answer the questions.

1. What is **matter**?

_____

_____

2. What are the three states, or forms, of matter?

_____

_____

3. What state of matter is a shoe?

_____

_____

4. How are solids and liquids different?

_____

_____

5. Liquids take the shape of . . .

_____

_____

6. What is an example of a gas?

_____

_____

7. Gold and iron are both examples of _____.

_____

_____

8. All matter is made up of _____.

_____

_____

Overview III: Introduction to
Opinion/Argument

What Is It?

What is an argument?

An argument is a way of writing that tries to convince readers to believe or do something. An argument has a strong point of view about an idea or a problem. It includes facts and examples to support an opinion, and it usually suggests a solution.

Examples

What are some examples of an argument?

- Essays
- Editorials
- Advertisements
- Letters
- Speeches
- Book and Film Reviews

Purpose

What is the purpose of an argument?

The writer wants the reader to:
- Change his or her mind;
- Act on something;
- Accept the writer's explanation.

Audience

Who is the audience for an argument?

The audience is anyone who the writer thinks he or she has a chance of persuading! The audience can be students, business leaders, politicians, or neighbors and friends.

How to Use It

How do you read an argument?

Ask yourself:
1. *What does the writer want or believe?*
2. *What does the writer think about it?*
3. *Does the writer give facts and good reasons?*
4. *Do I feel the same way as the writer or agree with the writer?*

What are some common features of an opinion/argument?

Tries to convince readers/audience to change mind or take action

Suggests solutions or actions

Conveys strong opinion or point of view

Opinion/ Argument

Targets specific reader/audience

Contains persuasive language

Contains facts/information to support opinion or point of view

Unit 8 Mini-Lesson
Persuasive Letters

What is a persuasive letter?

A persuasive letter is a letter that tries to convince readers to believe or do something. A persuasive letter has a strong point of view about an idea or a problem. It includes facts and examples to support an opinion, and it usually suggests a solution.

What is the purpose of a persuasive letter?

People write persuasive letters to "sway," or change the minds of, their readers. They want readers to see their points of view. They may want readers to take action, too.

Who is the audience for a persuasive letter?

People write persuasive letters to all kinds of people: parents, friends, citizens, business leaders, world leaders, and others. They write letters to make people understand their views. Often they want to change their audience's opinions. For example, someone might write to a leader about a law they don't agree with. The writer might want the leader to change the law.

How do you read a persuasive letter?

Keep in mind that the writer wants you to support his or her position. Ask yourself: *What is this writer's position, or opinion? Does he support it with facts and good reasons? Do I agree with him?* A good persuasive writer knows his audience. He knows what facts and reasons might change his reader's mind.

Unit 8 • *Common Core Comprehension Grade 4* • ©2012 Newmark Learning, LLC

Suggests solutions or actions

Has a strong position, or point of view

Has a specific audience in mind

Persuasive Letter

Uses powerful words to influence the reader

Uses facts and evidence to make a case

To the Editor:

As a parent, I strongly feel our town needs a new middle school. We need a new school more than we need a new mall. Our middle school is seventy years old. Truthfully, the school should be closed! The walls are falling down. Most classroom windows don't open. On hot days, our children **swelter** in the hot air. They suffer from the terrible heat. Two of the four children's bathrooms have been broken for six months. The Board of Education says there is no money to fix them. Last month, my daughter found a mouse crawling in her locker. The building is **infested**, or filled, with mice! Our middle school is a very big problem. Our children deserve better. Build a middle school where our children can feel safe.

Vivian Spencer

Dear Editor:

I'm okay with selling Old Oak Park to build a mall. But don't waste money on a new middle school. We already spend too much money on education. I pay two thousand dollars in taxes for the schools. I don't even have children! Our roads are a problem. We have more potholes than a war zone. Some of our streets have no lights at night. There is no public transportation. This makes life hard for our older and low-income residents. Let's form a city planning committee and improve the town for everyone.

Benjamin Taylor

To the Editor:

I'm the parent of a seventh grader. I feel strongly that our town needs a new middle school more than it needs a new mall. Our middle school is seventy years old, and frankly, it should be closed! The walls are crumbling. Most classroom windows don't open. On hot days, our children swelter in the stagnant, or still, air. The problem is more than the heat. Two of the four children's bathrooms have been out of commission, or not working, for six months. The Board of Education says there is no money to pay for the repairs. Last month, my daughter opened her locker. Inside was a mouse crawling on her backpack. The building is infested with mice. Our children deserve better. Sell the land and build a middle school where our children can feel safe.

Vivian Spencer

Dear Editor:

Sell Old Oak Park to build a mall, but please don't squander, or use up, my money on a new middle school. We already spend too much money on education in this community. I pay two thousand dollars in taxes to the local schools. I don't even have children! Our roads have more potholes than a war zone. Some of our streets have no lights at night. There is no public transportation. This hurts our older and low-income residents. Let's bring together a civic, or city, planning committee and improve the town for everyone.

Benjamin Taylor

To the Editor:

As the parent of a seventh grader, let me assure you this town needs a new middle school more than it needs a new mall. Our middle school is seventy years old, and it should be condemned! The walls are crumbling. Most classroom windows don't open. On hot days, our children swelter in the stagnant air. Two of the four children's bathrooms have been out of commission for six months. According to the Board of Education, no funds are available to pay for the repairs. Last month, my daughter opened her locker and found a mouse crawling on her backpack. The building is infested with mice. Our middle school is a disaster, and our children deserve better. Sell the land and build a middle school where our children can feel safe.

Vivian Spencer

Dear Editor:

Sell Old Oak Park to the mall developer, but please don't squander my money on a new middle school. We spend too much money on education in this community as it is. Almost two thousand dollars of my money goes to taxes to pay for local schools, and I don't even have children! Our roads have more potholes than a war zone. Some of our streets are not lighted at night. We have no public transportation system, which hurts our elderly and low-income residents. Let's bring together a civic planning committee and look for ways to improve the town for everyone.

Benjamin Taylor

Name _____ Date _____

Use what you read in the passage to answer the questions.

1. What does the word **swelter** mean?

_____

_____

2. How old is the middle school?

_____

_____

3. How are the writers' opinions different?

_____

_____

4. Why doesn't Benjamin Taylor think the money should be used to build a new school?

_____

_____

5. What is Vivian Spencer most upset about?

_____

_____

6. What does the word **infested** mean?

_____

_____

7. Why does Benjamin Taylor say that older and low-income residents have a hard time in this community?

_____

_____

8. Which writer do you think is most persuasive? Why?

_____

_____

Dear Editor:

Your story of Farmer Laurie shows that there is still a future in farming. Since 1990, seventy-eight percent of the small farmers in our state have stopped growing crops. Fifty-three percent of these small farmers have simply **abandoned** their land. They've just given it up. This is very upsetting. Farmer Laurie's solution is a great one. I am calling all farmers: Come back to our state! My administration will help. You will pay lower taxes. We will pay for research and education on organic farming. We will tell everyone about the benefits of organic foods. We can become a leader in the organic foods business. This was once a proud farming state. Let's look to a proud farming future as well.

Governor Leslie J. Tompkins

To the Editor:

I read your story about Laurie Sykes. Your newspaper has no idea what's happening in the real world. I have been out of work for more than a year. I don't care which fruit tastes better. I'm happy for my kids to get any fruit at all. I compared prices from Mega Mart and Farmer Laurie. Her prices are around a dollar more per pound on almost everything. I won't buy your paper ever again. I'll spend the money on fruit or vegetables. But I won't buy Farmer Laurie's food because it costs too much.

Mrs. Madeline McKnight

Dear Editor:

Farmer Laurie proves, or shows, that there's still a future in farming. Since 1990, seventy-eight percent of the small farmers in our state have stopped producing, or growing, crops. Fifty-three percent of these small farmers have simply abandoned, or given up, their land. Farmer Laurie proves you can still make a living from farming. I am calling all farmers: Let's start an organic farming revolution. My administration will help. We will provide tax relief, or a break on your taxes. We will pay for education on how to do organic farming. We will begin a campaign promoting, or "talking up," the benefits of organic foods. Our state can become a leader in organic foods. This was once a proud agricultural, or farming, state. Let's look to a proud farming future as well.

Governor Leslie J. Tompkins

To the Editor:

Your story about Laurie Sykes tells me that your newspaper has no idea what's happening in the real world. I have been out of work for more than a year. I don't care which fruit tastes better. I'm happy to get any fruit on a plate for my kids. I compared prices from Mega Mart and Farmer Laurie. Her prices are around a dollar more per pound on practically everything. Tomorrow I won't buy your paper. I won't buy it ever again. I will spend the money on fruit or vegetables. But I won't buy Farmer Laurie's food because it costs too much.

Mrs. Madeline McKnight

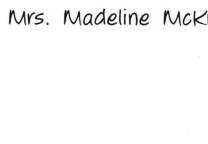

Dear Editor:

Laurie Sykes proves that there's still a future in farming. Since 1990, seventy-eight percent of the small farmers in our state have stopped producing crops. Fifty-three percent of these small farmers have simply abandoned their land and moved away. These are disturbing statistics. Farmer Laurie shows you can make a living off the land. I am calling all farmers: Let's start an organic farming revolution right here. My administration will provide tax relief to help you get started. We will support research and education on organic farming techniques. Together, our state can become a leader in the organic foods industry. This was once a proud agricultural state. Let's look to a proud farming future as well.

Governor Leslie J. Tompkins

To the Editor:

When I read your article on Laurie Sykes, I knew your paper was totally out of touch with reality. I have been out of work for more than a year. I can tell you that people don't care which fruit tastes better. We're happy to get any fruit on a plate for our kids. I compared prices from Mega Mart and Farmer Laurie. Her prices are around a dollar more per pound. Tomorrow I won't be buying your paper. In fact, I won't ever buy it again. I'm going to spend the money on fruit or vegetables—but not Farmer Laurie's, because they cost too much.

Mrs. Madeline McKnight

●●●

Name _____ Date _____

Use what you read in the passage to answer the questions.

1. What does the word **abandoned** mean in this passage?

_____

_____

2. What percentage of farmers have abandoned their land?

_____

_____

3. What is Governor Tompkins trying to convince or persuade farmers to do?

_____

_____

4. What clues in Mrs. McKnight's letter help you conclude organic fruit is expensive?

_____

_____

5. Why won't Mrs. McKnight buy the paper anymore?

_____

_____

6. What are the facts in Governor Tompkins's letter?

_____

_____

7. What are the facts in Mrs. McKnight's letter?

_____

_____

8. Which letter is in support of organic farming?

_____

_____

Unit 9 Mini-Lesson
Film/Book Reviews

What is a film or book review?

A film or book review is a summary of comments and opinions about a book or film. The writer tells what happens in the story and shares his or her opinions about it. The writer tells what is good about the book or film and what might be bad or weak. The writer uses details to support his or her opinions.

What is the purpose of a film or book review?

People write reviews to share with others the joys of books or films. Many people like to know about a book or movie before they read it or watch it. That way, they know if the book or film is a right match for them. Does the subject interest them?

Who is the audience for a film or book review?

The audience for the review depends on the audience for the book or film, as well as the audience where the review will be printed. The audience will be people interested in that subject. The reviewer writes to all of the people who might want to read the book or see the film that he or she is reviewing.

How do you read a film or book review?

Pay attention to the plot, characters, and subject matter. Does the story line appeal to you? Did it interest the reviewer? How can you tell? What did the reviewer like? What did the reviewer dislike? Did he or she give good reasons for his or her opinions? Do you want to read the book or see the film now?

Describes the main setting, main characters, and basic plot of the story

Gives the title and information about the author or actors

Does NOT give away any surprises or the ending

Film or Book Review

Includes short quotes from the book or film to illustrate a point

Gives opinions on the strengths and weaknesses

Skip This *Peter Pan*

Don't see the musical movie of *Peter Pan*. This is a movie of the Broadway musical that was performed live on TV in 1960. But it isn't nearly as good.

Peter Pan is the story of a boy who won't grow up. He lives with other Lost Boys. They live on an island called Neverland. The island has pirates. The sneaky Captain Hook leads the pirates. Hook has his name because he has a hook instead of a hand.

One night, Peter flies away from Neverland. He sneaks into the home of the Darling family. He teaches Wendy and her brothers how to fly. They fly to Neverland. That's when a whole lot of trouble begins. Captain Hook wants to kill Peter. Hook hates Peter Pan for cutting off his hand in a fight.

Captain Hook was the only character I really liked. You might think he'd be threatening, but he's not. He is actually cowardly! He is also playful in the role. He made me laugh out loud. He's the best Captain Hook I have ever seen!

Mary Martin is Peter Pan. A woman has always played the part of Peter. That's because the songs have very high notes. Most male actors can't sing them. Martin is a great singer and dancer. She acts well, too. But she is too old to be Peter Pan. It's impossible to believe she's a boy. If you see the movie, I bet you'll agree.

There are other *Peter Pan* movies. They are all pretty good. But few of the others are full musicals, like this one. If you want to hear the songs, you can go see this movie. But I have a better idea: Skip the movie and just listen to the CD.

● ○ ○

Skip This *Peter Pan*

I don't recommend seeing the musical movie of *Peter Pan*. This is a version of the Broadway musical that was performed live on TV in 1960. But it isn't very good.

Peter Pan is the story of a boy who won't grow up. He lives with other Lost Boys on an island called Neverland. The island has pirates. They are led by the dastardly, or not so nice, Captain Hook. He has that name because he has a hook instead of a hand.

One night, Peter flies away from Neverland. He sneaks into the home of the Darling family. He teaches Wendy and her brothers how to fly. After they fly to Neverland, a whole lot of trouble begins. Captain Hook wants to kill Peter. Hook hates the boy for cutting off his hand in a fight.

The only character I really liked was Captain Hook. You might expect him to be threatening, but he's not. He is playful and cowardly. He made me laugh out loud. He's the best Captain Hook I have ever seen!

Mary Martin is Peter Pan. A woman plays the part of Peter because the songs have very high notes. Most male actors can't sing them. Martin is a talented singer and dancer. She acts well, too. But she is too old to play the part of Peter Pan. It's impossible to believe she's a boy. See the movie. I bet you'll agree.

There are other *Peter Pan* movies. A few of them are animated, or cartoons. Others have live characters. They are all pretty good. But few of the others are full musicals, like this one. If you want to hear the songs, you can go see this movie. But I have a better idea: Skip the movie and just listen to the CD.

Skip This *Peter Pan*

Think twice before watching this musical version of *Peter Pan*. This version of the Broadway musical that was performed live on TV in 1960 just doesn't pack much punch.

Peter Pan is the story of a boy who won't grow up. He lives on an island called Neverland with other Lost Boys. The island has pirates led by the dastardly Captain Hook, so named because he has a hook instead of a hand.

One night, Peter flies away from Neverland. He sneaks into the home of the Darling family. He teaches Wendy and her brothers how to fly. After they fly to Neverland, a whole lot of trouble begins. Captain Hook is on a mission to kill Peter. Hook hates the boy for cutting off his hand in a fight.

The only character I really liked was Captain Hook. Captain Hook is bossy but not as threatening as you might expect. He is playful—and cowardly. He made me laugh out loud. He's the best Captain Hook I have ever seen!

Mary Martin plays Peter Pan. A woman plays the role of Peter for a reason. The songs have very high notes. Most male actors can't sing them. Martin is a talented singer and dancer. She acts well, too. But she is far too old for this role. It's impossible to believe she's a boy. See the movie yourself and I bet you'll agree.

There are several other *Peter Pan* movies. A few of them are animated. Others have live characters. They are all pretty good. But few of the others are full-scale musicals. If you want to see the songs performed, then go ahead and watch this movie. But I have a better idea: Skip the movie and just listen to the CD.

Name _____ Date _____

Use what you read in the passage to answer the questions.

1. What movie is being reviewed?

_____

_____

2. Where does Peter Pan live?

_____

_____

3. What does Peter Pan teach Wendy and her brothers?

_____

_____

4. Why does Captain Hook want to kill Peter?

_____

_____

5. What clue tells you that the reviewer thinks Captain Hook is funny?

_____

_____

6. What part does Mary Martin play?

_____

_____

7. Why would it be hard for a male actor to play the part of Peter Pan?

_____

_____

8. Why did the reviewer title the review "Skip This *Peter Pan*"?

_____

_____

The Princess and the Pea

The Princess and the Pea is funny. It is not a regular fairy tale. It breaks the rules. You could even say it is silly! Hans Christian Andersen is the author. The tale was published in 1835. He thought people would like the story. Well, he was right about that! Everyone will enjoy this story.

The plot of *The Princess and the Pea* is impossible. You might say it is **preposterous**. A prince travels the world looking for a real princess. The prince cannot find a proper lady. The author makes it sound as if the prince goes shopping. But instead of buying stuff, he is shopping for a wife!

The prince doesn't have a good shopping trip. Readers must guess why. Is the prince too picky? Does he not know what to look for?

The author never really lets us get to know the prince. But that's part of the fun. All we know is that the prince comes home sad. He comes home without a princess.

Then things get really interesting! One stormy night, there's a knock at the castle door. A young woman arrives. She is standing in the rain. She says she is a princess. But this princess is a mess. She has dripping hair. Her clothes and shoes are wet. The queen is not sure this woman is a princess. So she makes up a test. Can you guess from the title what happens? The test involves a pea and mattresses. Will the princess pass the test? Read the story and find out. You won't be disappointed.

The Princess and the Pea

The Princess and the Pea is not your typical fairy tale. This one breaks the rules. In fact, you could even say it's goofy. Hans Christian Andersen published the tale in 1835. He thought it would amuse people. Well, he was right about that! Everyone will enjoy this story.

The plot of *The Princess and the Pea* is downright preposterous. A prince has roamed the world looking for a real princess. "He traveled all over the world to find one," writes Andersen, "but nowhere could he get what he sought." Andersen makes it sound as though princes go shopping for their princesses. He is obviously having fun with the fairy tale genre.

Apparently this prince doesn't have a very successful shopping spree. "Each young lady always had something about her that was not as it should be," explains Andersen. Readers must draw their own conclusions about why. Is the prince too picky? Does he not know what to look for?

The writer never really lets us get to know the prince. The story doesn't have a lot of character development. But that's part of the fun. All we know is that the prince comes home empty-handed and sad.

Then things get really interesting! One stormy night, there's a knock at the castle door. A young woman is standing outside in the pouring rain. She claims to be a princess. But this princess is a mess—from her dripping hair and clothes to her soggy shoes! The queen is not sure this woman is really a princess so she creates a test. As you can guess from the title, this test involves a pea. The test also involves twenty mattresses. Will the princess pass the test? Read the story and find out. You won't be disappointed.

The Princess and the Pea

The Princess and the Pea is not your typical fairy tale. If you are accustomed to fairy tales, this one breaks the rules. In fact, you could even say it's goofy. Hans Christian Andersen published the tale in 1835. He thought it would amuse people. Well, he was absolutely right about that! Everyone will enjoy this story.

The plot of *The Princess and the Pea* is downright preposterous. A prince has roamed the world searching high and low for a real princess. "He traveled all over the world to find one," writes Andersen, "but nowhere could he get what he sought." Andersen makes it sound as though princes go shopping for their princesses. He is obviously having fun with the fairy tale genre.

Apparently this prince doesn't have a very successful shopping spree. "Each young lady always had something about her that was not as it should be," explains Andersen. Readers must draw their own conclusions about why. Is the prince too picky? Should he have settled for any young princess? What are the qualifications of a princess?

The writer never really lets us get to know the prince. The story is lacking in character development. But that's part of the fun. All we know is that the prince comes home empty-handed and dejected.

Then things get really interesting! One stormy night, there's a knock at the castle door. A young woman is standing outside in the pouring rain. She claims to be a princess, but this princess is a mess! The queen is not sure this woman is really a princess, so she devises a test. As you can guess from the title, this test involves a pea. The test also involves twenty mattresses. Will the princess pass the test? Read the story and find out. You won't be disappointed.

Name _____ Date _____

Use what you read in the passage to answer the questions.

1. Who wrote the original tale *The Princess and the Pea*?

_____

_____

2. What does the word **preposterous** mean in the story?

_____

_____

3. Does the reviewer like this story? Give an example from the text to support your view.

_____

_____

4. Why doesn't the prince choose a princess right away?

_____

_____

5. What happens on a stormy night?

_____

_____

6. Why doesn't the queen believe the girl is a princess?

_____

_____

7. Does this story seem like something that could happen in real life? Why or why not?

_____

_____

8. What prediction can you make about how the story ends? Explain your answer.

_____

_____

Unit 10 Mini-Lesson
Advertisements

What is an advertisement?

An advertisement, or "ad," is a form of persuasive communication. It may include writing, images, or both. For written ads, the copywriter tries to persuade his or her audience to buy or do something. The writer tells what is good about a product or service. The writer also tries to persuade people that they need this product or service.

What is the purpose of an advertisement?

People write advertisements to sell products. The goal of an ad is to persuade others to buy or use certain goods or services. Ads often explain how a product or service can help solve a problem or make people's lives better. Often, ads try to entertain people, or make a lasting impression in some way so that people will remember to buy the product.

Who is the audience for an advertisement?

The audience for an advertisement is the consumer, or person who buys things. The specific consumer audience depends on the product or service being sold. It also depends on where the ad is printed. The audience will be people interested in that product.

How do you read an advertisement?

1. Look to see what product or service is being sold.
2. Ask yourself whether the ad writer does a good job of selling.
3. Does the ad leave a lasting impression on you?
4. Does the writer convince you that you want or perhaps even need the product? If yes, what did the writer say that convinced you?

Describes why a product or service is worth buying/using

Targets a specific consumer audience based on where the ad is presented

Gives the name and information about a product and where to buy it

Gives opinions on the strengths of a product or service

Advertisement

May include any of the following text structures: description, main idea and supporting facts and details, compare and contrast, problem/solution, cause and effect

May include endorsements, awards, or notable mentions that the product has won

Leaves a lasting impression so consumers will want to buy the product

Fog Horn

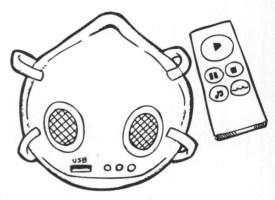

If you live with a person who snores, you know how hard it is to fall asleep. Are you tired of listening to snoring every night? Is your snoring roommate keeping you awake? Do you need a good night's sleep? Do you hear the snoring even when you wear earplugs?

Everyone deserves a good night's sleep. Now you can get one, too! Fog Horn is a brand-new anti-snoring machine. Fog Horn hides the sounds of snoring. Your nights of lying awake listening to snoring are over. Now you can fall asleep to the peaceful sounds of nature. Fog Horn does not drown out the sounds of snoring. Instead, it uses the vibrations caused by snoring. The vibrations send sounds that you choose.

Fog Horn is easy to use. Put the Fog Horn mask over the snorer's mouth and nose. Fog Horn is comfortable to wear. It fits on the face with special memory foam padding. The wearer will not even notice it's on. Then choose from several nature sounds. "Rain Forest" is animal sounds. "Ocean" is the sound of gentle waves and seagulls.

You also have the choice of listening to your own music. Upload your favorite songs to Fog Horn and fall asleep to music. Adjust the volume with the remote control. Simply choose a volume that will take you to dreamland. With Fog Horn, every night is a good night's sleep. And you'll wake up every morning refreshed.

Get Fog Horn today and sleep peacefully tonight.

Fog Horn

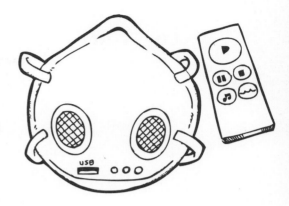

We all know that feeling. You know— the one when you're ready to go to sleep for the night but you can't. Why? Because the person in the room with you is snoring like a chainsaw! Are you tired of listening to snoring? Do you need a good night's sleep? Is your snoring roommate keeping you up? Do you hear the snoring even with earplugs in?

Everyone deserves a good night's sleep, and now you can get one. Fog Horn is the newest anti-snoring product to hit the market. Fog Horn hides the sounds of snoring. It replaces the noise of snoring with more peaceful sounds so you can fall asleep. Fog Horn does not drown out the sounds of snoring. Instead, it uses the vibrations caused by snoring. The vibrations send programmed sounds that you choose.

Fog Horn is easy to use. Put the Fog Horn mask over the snorer's mouth and nose. Select among several soothing sounds. "Rain Forest" has a soft background of animal sounds. "Ocean" is the sound of gentle waves and seagulls. Fog Horn is comfortable to wear. It fits on the face with special memory foam padding. The wearer will not even notice.

Fog Horn comes with a USB port. A USB port lets you connect the mask to your music. Upload your favorite songs and fall asleep to music of your choice. Fog Horn has a remote control to adjust the volume. Choose a volume that will take you to dreamland. With Fog Horn, every night is a good night's sleep. And you'll wake up in the morning feeling refreshed.

Finally, a product that gives you control of your sleep. Get Fog Horn today and sleep peacefully tonight.

Fog Horn

We have all been there before. You are ready to lie down for a peaceful night's sleep when a loud noise coming from the other person in the room shatters the quiet. Are you tired of listening to the other person in the room snore? Need a good night's sleep? Is your noisy roommate keeping you up with his or her snoring? Do earplugs not drown out the loud noise?

Solve your sleeping problems with the Fog Horn. Fog Horn is the newest sleeping sensation to hit the market. Fog Horn disguises one's snores to create a more pleasant noise to fall asleep to. Fog Horn does not drown out the sounds of snoring. Instead it uses the vibrations caused by snoring to transmit programmed sounds instead of a loud snoring noise.

Simply place the Fog Horn mask over the mouth and nose of the snorer. Select your setting and sleep to a soothing noise. Fog Horn sits comfortably on the face with special memory foam padding. The wearer will not even notice it. Fog Horn has several settings to choose from in order to have a soothing night's sleep. Choose "Rain Forest" to fall asleep to the soft background of animal sounds. Choose "Ocean" to dream of days sleeping on the beach.

Fog Horn also comes with a USB port, which allows you to connect the mask to your music. Upload your favorite songs and fall asleep to the music you choose. Fog Horn even has a remote that allows you to adjust the volume so that you can drift to dreamland in peace.

Fog Horn allows you to get a good night's sleep and wake up in the morning feeling refreshed. Finally, a product gives you the peace and tranquility to sleep to the background noise you choose. Get Fog Horn today and start sleeping peacefully tonight.

Name _____ Date _____

Use what you read in the passage to answer the questions.

1. What is this an advertisement for?

_____

_____

2. What problem does Fog Horn solve?

_____

_____

3. How does Fog Horn work?

_____

_____

4. Who wears Fog Horn?

_____

_____

5. What clues let you know the Fog Horn is comfortable to wear?

_____

_____

6. What two types of sounds does Fog Horn offer?

_____

_____

7. What does Fog Horn promise the user?

_____

_____

8. Would you buy Fog Horn? Why or why not?

_____

_____

Glow Sports

The sun sets. It's the end of a warm spring day. You want to keep playing ball, but it's dark. You can't see a thing. Do your sports practices end early just because the sun has set? With Glow Sports you can make outdoor playtime last longer. Glow Sports provides a full range of sporting equipment that glows in the dark. Glow Sports allows for hours of nighttime fun.

Who needs stadium lights to play ball at night? The Glow Sports baseball kit comes with glow-in-the-dark baseballs, bats, and bases. It even includes glow-in-the-dark jerseys and hats. The Glow Sports soccer kit includes a glow-in-the-dark soccer ball, goals, and cones. What's your favorite sport? Whatever sport you play, there is a Glow Sports kit—basketball, football, and lacrosse, to name a few. With each set, you will also receive glow-in-the-dark tape to mark your playing field. The tape sticks easily to any surface.

Glow Sports is perfect for sports training in the colder months when days are shorter. Schedule practices whenever you want. Don't worry about rushing through a practice before it gets dark.

Glow Sports makes high-level sporting equipment that is built to last and built to glow. Glow Sports offers complete sets or individual equipment. You can find Glow Sports wherever sporting equipment is sold. Glow Sports is ready for all your late-night sporting needs. Who needs the sun? Get outside and keep the game glowing.

Glow Sports

The sun sets at the end of a warm spring day. You want to keep playing ball, but you can't see a thing! Do your sports teams end practice before you want just because the light is fading? Well, it's time to extend outdoor playtime! Glow Sports makes it possible for you to play outside long after the sun has gone down. Glow Sports provides a full range of sporting equipment that glows in the dark to allow you hours of nighttime fun.

Who needs stadium lights to play ball at night? The Glow Sports baseball kit comes with glow-in-the-dark baseballs, bats, and bases. It even includes glow-in-the-dark jerseys and hats. The Glow Sports soccer kit includes a glow-in-the-dark soccer ball, portable goals, and cones. What's your favorite sport? Whatever sport you play—basketball, football, lacrosse—there is a Glow Sports kit for you. With each set, you will also receive glow-in-the-dark tape to mark your playing field. The tape sticks easily to any surface.

Glow Sports is ideal for sports training in the colder months when daylight can be sparse. Schedule practices whenever you choose. Don't worry about rushing through a practice to beat the sunlight.

Glow Sports makes high-level sporting equipment that is built to last and built to glow. Glow Sports offers complete sets or individual equipment. You can find Glow Sports wherever sporting equipment is sold. Glow Sports is ready for all your late-night sporting needs. Who needs the sun? Get outside and keep the game glowing.

Glow Sports

It's the end of the day and the last thing you want to do is hide inside because the sun is down. Do your sports teams have to end practice early because the light is fading? It's impossible to play outside without sunlight, right? Well, it's time to extend

outdoor playtime! Don't sit around and wait for the sun to come up! Go outside and play with Glow Sports. Glow Sports includes a full range of sporting equipment that glows in the dark to allow you hours of nighttime fun. Glow Sports includes glow-in-the-dark soccer balls, baseballs, basketballs, and footballs. Each Glow Sports sets include glow-in-the-dark scrimmage jerseys to play with all your friends.

Use the Glow Sports baseball packet to play a late night baseball game. The packet includes glow-in-the-dark baseballs, bats, bases, and hats. The Glow Sports soccer kit includes a glow-in-the-dark soccer ball, portable goals, and cones. Each of the sets also includes glow-in-the-dark tape to mark your playing field. The tape easily rolls out onto any surface and rolls back up for multiple uses.

Glow Sports is ideal for sports training in the colder months when daylight can be sparse. Schedule practices whenever you choose. Don't worry about rushing through a practice to beat the sunlight. Glow Sports makes high-level sporting equipment that is built to last and built to glow. Buy Glow Sports kits or buy individual equipment. If you need a Glow Sports soccer ball and scrimmage vest, simply go to your nearest store and look for the equipment sold individually. Glow Sports is ready for all your late-night sporting needs. Who needs the sun? Get outside and keep the game glowing.

Name _____ Date _____

Use what you read in the passage to answer the questions.

1. What is this advertisement selling?

_____

_____

2. Who is this advertisement meant for?

_____

_____

3. What does the Glow Sports baseball kit include?

_____

_____

4. At what time of day is Glow Sports meant to be used? Why?

_____

_____

5. Why might you need glow-in-the-dark tape?

_____

_____

6. Why is Glow Sports good for colder months?

_____

_____

7. Where can you buy Glow Sports?

_____

_____

8. Glow Sports come in complete sets or _____.

_____

_____

Answer Key

Unit 1 Personal Narratives I
page 13

1. San Diego, California
2. A black convertible. It is awesome because the top can be put down.
3. Nicer because the beach in Corpus Christi has brown water filled with seaweed
4. No. The writer says so.
5. Bright yellow and pink with fish swimming around
6. A fish swims right under the narrator's hand.
7. The size of a half-dollar
8. Lucky to have had that adventure. The writer says so.

Unit 1 Personal Narratives II
page 17

1. Lucy is a dog.
2. A business trip
3. Because she thinks her dog is going to be put to sleep
4. Dr. Malden
5. Back problems
6. Because Lucy is heavy to carry to the car
7. In her bedroom
8. Answers will vary.

Unit 2 Realistic Fiction I
page 23

1. Nineteenth-century western pioneers
2. Jamal says he doesn't want to do Luke's work for him.
3. Two pages
4. Spinning wheel
5. Tia
6. They attacked the pioneers and ate all the pioneers' food.
7. He is surprised by how many books there are in the set.
8. He finds the book with the letter *P* and looks up *pioneer*.

Unit 2 Realistic Fiction II
page 27

1. Can take it different places
2. The bongo drums
3. He can't play an instrument.
4. She is scared of the cave. She looks for an excuse not to practice there.
5. It will make the music sound better.
6. So the kids can see one another in the dark
7. A miner's light. His dad got it at an antique store.
8. The clicking from his light becomes his instrument.

Answer Key

Unit 3 Historical Fiction I
page 33

1. A famous Spanish explorer
2. Florida
3. Answers will vary.
4. Ten years old
5. An old person who swims in it becomes young again.
6. The tribe because it outnumbered the Spanish and poisoned Ponce de León with an arrow
7. Answers will vary.
8. By going bravely through life

Unit 3 Historical Fiction II
page 37

1. 1757
2. She stomped out the front door.
3. They both like to read.
4. Because she can't go to school like the boys
5. *Romeo and Juliet* by William Shakespeare
6. He wanted to borrow a book from Reverend Smith.
7. Because they get to go to school and learn
8. He was friendly and helped lift her spirits.

Unit 4 Trickster Tales I
page 43

1. Keeping things to yourself and not sharing
2. On a mountaintop
3. Because they suffer in the winter without any fire
4. Squirrel, Chipmunk, and Frog
5. Squirrel
6. The fire scorches her back and her tail curls up in pain.
7. Onto a piece of wood
8. They screech with anger.

Unit 4 Trickster Tales II
page 47

1. Milk
2. Because Sis Cow replied angrily that she would not give him any milk
3. Run into the tree
4. Unable to move
5. To get Sis Cow's milk
6. So she can trick Brer Rabbit
7. Sis Cow will treat Brer Rabbit the same way he had treated her.
8. A deep, disguised voice

Answer Key

Unit 5 Pourquoi Tales I
page 53

1. Because it snowed for a long time
2. To the south
3. He kicks his boot heels together and they float up into the sky.
4. It makes fire and shows her power to the stars.
5. Because their families left, and they are alone
6. Brother makes the loudest sound on Earth with his boots.
7. "Like a knife through butter"
8. Why there is lightning and thunder

Unit 5 Pourquoi Tales II
page 57

1. Making things or actions seem bigger than they could possibly be
2. Two leaves; because he didn't want to listen to Mosquito
3. Because he was frightened when Snake rushed in
4. She shouts, "Danger!"
5. Crow's warning
6. Upset. She says she will never again wake up the sun.
7. Because the sun did not come up that day
8. Buzzing in people's ears

Unit 6 Civilizations of the Americas
page 65

1. The nobles
2. Commoners
3. One was for boys to learn how to farm and be soldiers and for girls to learn how to cook and raise children. The other was for boys to learn to become priests or leaders.
4. Nobles
5. Farming
6. Corn, beans, and squash
7. They traded food and other things.
8. Answers will vary.

Unit 6 Geography and Climate
page 69

1. Mountains, valleys, rivers, lakes, and seacoasts
2. They have eroded.
3. The United States and Canada
4. They act like a wall.
5. It is known for its great beaches and fishing.
6. Lake Erie and Lake Ontario
7. It has a tall, wide waterfall.
8. The Atlantic Ocean

Common Core Comprehension Grade 4 • ©2012 Newmark Learning, LLC

Answer Key

Unit 6 Economics
page 73

1. Athens, Greece
2. Main cities and areas around them
3. Athens was named for Athena.
4. An outdoor market
5. Greek soil is thin, and it doesn't always rain.
6. Bread
7. Democracy
8. Through its art, literature, ideas, and democracy

Unit 6 Native Americans
page 77

1. Horses
2. Hunters could follow the buffalo herds easier.
3. They could use the buffalo for almost everything they needed.
4. Groups of Comanche
5. Roots or buffalo
6. People who wander
7. Through games and chores
8. Answers will vary.

Unit 7 Life Science: Organisms
page 83

1. Plants
2. More than 400,000
3. Both have cells.
4. Tells the cell what to do
5. It gives a plant its shape and holds the plant straight up.
6. Chlorophyll
7. A gas that plants use to make food
8. We give plants carbon dioxide for food and they give us oxygen to breathe.

Unit 7 Life Science: Classification
page 87

1. Classification
2. Kingdom
3. On the outside of its body
4. Arthropods
5. Spinal cords
6. Vertebrates have backbones and invertebrates don't.
7. Class
8. Family

Answer Key

Unit 7 Earth Science
page 91

1. Many buildings fell, people died, and the city burned for days.
2. The crust
3. Cracks in Earth's crust
4. The plates push hard against the rocks.
5. Because earthquakes are likely to happen again in the same faults
6. 1811 and 1812
7. An earthquake deep in the Indian Ocean
8. They had no warning.

Unit 7 Physical Science
page 95

1. Anything that takes up space and has mass
2. Solid, liquid, and gas
3. Solid
4. Solids have a shape but liquids take the shape of their containers. Liquids can also be poured.
5. Whatever they're in
6. Answers will vary.
7. Elements
8. Elements

Unit 8 Persuasive Letters I
page 103

1. To suffer from the hot air
2. Seventy years old
3. Answers will vary.
4. Enough money is already spent on education.
5. The bad condition of the middle school
6. Full of some kind of pest or dangerous animals
7. There is no public transportation.
8. Answers will vary.

Unit 8 Persuasive Letters II
page 107

1. Moved out without selling
2. Fifty-three percent
3. To come back to the state to be trained in organic farming
4. Farmer Laurie's prices are a dollar more per pound.
5. Because she can barely afford even basic food
6. Seventy-eight percent of the small farmers have stopped growing crops. Fifty-three percent of these small farmers have abandoned their land.
7. Farmer Laurie's prices are a dollar more per pound than Mega Mart's prices.
8. Governor Leslie Tompkins's

Common Core Comprehension Grade 4 • ©2012 Newmark Learning, LLC

Answer Key

Unit 9 Film Reviews
page 113

1. *Peter Pan*
2. The island Neverland
3. How to fly
4. Peter cut off Hook's hand.
5. Captain Hook makes him laugh out loud.
6. Peter Pan
7. A male actor couldn't sing the high notes.
8. Because the reviewer does not like it

Unit 9 Book Reviews
page 117

1. Hans Christian Andersen
2. Impossible; foolish
3. Yes. The writer says, "Everyone will enjoy this story."
4. There is something he doesn't like about each princess he meets.
5. A princess arrives at the castle.
6. She looks messy.
7. Answers will vary.
8. Answers will vary.

Unit 10 Advertisements I
page 123

1. Fog Horn
2. Helps you sleep while someone is snoring
3. Using vibrations from snoring and changing it to pleasant sounds
4. People who are snoring
5. It fits on the face with memory foam padding.
6. Rain Forest and Ocean
7. A good night's sleep
8. Answers will vary.

Unit 10 Advertisements II
page 127

1. Glow Sports
2. People who play sports outside
3. Glow-in-the-dark baseballs, bats, bases, jerseys, and hats
4. Nighttime because the equipment glows in the dark
5. To mark the field you are playing on
6. Because that's when the days are shorter and there's less daylight
7. Wherever sporting equipment is sold
8. Individual equipment

Notes

Notes